Jungle Serenade

Rainforest Rhythms

Rafeal Mechlore

Leader Enterprises

Jungle Serenade

CONTENTS

INDEX 1

INTRODUCTION 3

Chapter 1 16

Chapter 2 31

Chapter 3 47

Chapter 4 63

Chapter 5 75

Chapter 6 90

Chapter 7 105

Chapter 8 119

Chapter 9 135

INDEX

Introduction

1. Definition of Animal Symbolism
2. Importance of Animals in Mythology
3. Purpose and Scope of the Book
4. Methodology and Approach

Chapter 1 The Significance of Animals in Human Culture
1.1 Historical Overview
1.2 Psychological and Cultural Significance
1.3 Animals in Prehistoric Art and Religion

Chapter 2 Animals as Totems and Spirits
2.1 Totemism: Ancestral Connections
2.2 Guardian Spirits and Familiars
2.3 Animal Spirits in Shamanism

Chapter 3 The Cosmic Menagerie: Animals in Creation Myths
3.1 World-Forming Beasts
3.2 Animal Deities and their Roles in Creation
3.3 Origin Stories and Animal Archetypes

Chapter 4 Metaphorical Menageries: Animals as Symbols
4.1 Animals as Representations of Virtues and Vices
4.2 Cultural Variations in Symbolism
4.3 The Universal Language of Animal Metaphors

Chapter 5 Beasts in Divine Guise: Anthropomorphic Deities
5.1 Gods and Goddesses with Animal Attributes
5.2 The Concept of Zoomorphism

5.3Divine Shapeshifters and Hybrid Beings

Chapter 6 Animals in Rituals and Ceremonies
6.1Sacrificial Animals and Ritualistic Practices
6.2Animal Festivals and Celebrations
6.3The Role of Animals in Divination

Chapter 7 Folklore and Fables: Animal Stories and Morality Tales
7.1Aesop's Fables and Animal Morality
7.2Beast Epics in World Literature
7.3Lessons from Animal Narratives

Chapter 8 Myths, Ecology, and Conservation
8.1Indigenous Wisdom and Environmental Ethics
8.2Animals in Modern Ecology and Conservation Movements
8.3The Relevance of Animal Mythology in Contemporary Environmental Issues

Chapter 9 The Legacy of Animal Symbolism in Art, Literature, and Popular Culture
9.1Animal Motifs in Artistic Expression
9.2Animals in Contemporary Literature and Media
9.3The Ever-Evolving Role of Animals in Modern Culture

INTRODUCTION

Creatures have long held a focal and persevering through place in the embroidery of human culture and conviction frameworks. These animals, both homegrown and wild, have woven their direction into our accounts, ceremonies, and awareness, rising above topographical, fleeting, and social limits. The strong imagery and folklore related with creatures have given mankind a common language to communicate complex thoughts, values, and feelings. From the old cavern canvases of Lascaux to the perplexing pictographs of old Egypt, from the awe-inspiring accounts of the world's extraordinary religions to the advanced tales that engage and educate, creatures have been our associates, our instructors, and our images.

The reason for this book, "Monsters and Convictions: Creature Imagery and Folklore Across Societies," is to set out on an excursion through the huge and many-sided domain of creature imagery and folklore. Inside these pages, we will unwind the strings of implying that people have woven around creatures for centuries, investigate the assorted manners by which creatures have been coordinated into the profound and social scenes of various social orders, and examine the meaning of this getting through relationship.

Why have creatures enthralled human creative mind for such a long time? What do these animals address, and how have they helped shape how we might interpret the world and our place inside it? These inquiries lie at the core of our investigation, and we will start by characterizing our terms and making way for our excursion.

The Importance of Creature Imagery

Creature imagery can be comprehensively characterized as the attribution of emblematic or allegorical implications to explicit creatures or gatherings of creatures. This training reaches out across assorted societies and developments and has advanced north of millennia. The implications credited to creatures can shift broadly, enveloping a range of characteristics, both positive and negative, and frequently mirror the specific social, geological, or verifiable setting in which they are found.

The meaning of creatures in representative language is well established in human comprehension and feeling. Creatures are a piece of our day to day routines and have made a permanent imprint on our shared perspective. They are essential to our nearby climate as pets, bugs, or untamed life, and they have involved a conspicuous spot in the social and mental scene of mankind. Thusly, creature imagery is a rich and dynamic feature of human experience that illuminates our qualities, legends, and customs.

The universality of creature imagery emerges from the significant associations among people and the set of all animals. From early agrarian social orders to present day metropolitan places, our lives have been unpredictably entwined with creatures. They have given food, attire, and apparatuses, however they have likewise filled in as wellsprings of motivation, dread, and secret. These multi-layered connections have led to a huge range of implications credited to creatures. As we investigate the different parts of creature imagery in this book, we will experience the numerous jobs creatures have played in the human mind and culture.

Creatures in Folklore: Watchmen of the Human Soul

Folklore, similar to creature imagery, is a fundamental piece of human culture. Fanciful stories, beginning from different societies all over the planet, act as the other-worldly and moral compass of social orders, giving accounts that make sense of the starting points of the world, the idea of humankind, and the powers that administer our lives. Inside these fantasies, creatures frequently become the dominant focal point, encapsulating complex original characteristics and profound aspects.

Creatures in folklore are not simply latent images; they are dynamic specialists in the unfurling show of human life. They exemplify our apprehensions, wants, and desires, offering direction and showing important illustrations. Whether through awe-inspiring stories or moral tales, creatures are focal characters in the narratives that assist us with exploring the intricacies of life.

This book will dive into the significant universe of creature folklore, analyzing the jobs creatures play in the making of the universe, the development of social character, and the statement of profound convictions. We will uncover the different manners by which creatures have been worshipped as divine beings, goddesses, and guardian angels, or castigated as malicious powers. Through these fanciful accounts, we will acquire knowledge into the human longing to interface with the normal world, to grasp our place inside it, and to look for amazing quality through the animals of the world collectively.

The Reason and Extent of Our Investigation

Our investigation of creature imagery and folklore is a diverse and interdisciplinary excursion. We will cross mainlands and hundreds of years, winding around together strings of information from different customs, including old, native, and contemporary conviction frameworks. This variety mirrors the intricacy of human associations with the set of all animals and highlights the all inclusiveness of the human-creature association.

All through this book, we will look at the meaning of creatures as emblems and gatekeeper spirits, investigate their parts in creation fantasies, disentangle the layers of figurative implications credited to them, and dig into the possibility of human gods that obscure the limits among people and creatures. We will likewise consider the vital job creatures play in customs and functions, both in antiquated and present day settings.

Besides, we will investigate how creatures have been highlighted in old stories, tales, and writing, filling in as vehicles for moral and philosophical lessons. We will likewise examine the significant impact of creature imagery on workmanship, writing, and mainstream society, featuring its proceeded with importance in the contemporary world.

Our investigation won't be restricted to the past or the hypothetical; we will likewise inspect how the tradition of creature imagery and folklore has molded contemporary biological and protection developments. The insight contained in native convictions, as well as the experiences got from antiquated folklores, can offer significant illustrations for tending to the natural difficulties within recent memory.

Strategy and Approach

To explore the sweeping and multifaceted domain of creature imagery and folklore, our methodology will be multidisciplinary and comprehensive. We will draw on the areas of humanities, relative religion, social examinations, legends, and ecological investigations to give an extensive perspective regarding this matter. Our technique will consolidate a large number of sources, including old texts, oral practices, craftsmanship, and writing, as well as contemporary scholastic examination and biological talk.

We perceive that each culture has its own novel viewpoint on creature imagery and folklore. Thusly, we expect to give a decent investigation of these different perspectives while likewise distinguishing the all inclusive subjects and examples that arise. The accounts and images of native societies are no less pertinent than those of additional broadly perceived social orders, and we will endeavor to approach all points of view with deference and responsiveness.

As we set out on this excursion through the universe of creature imagery and folklore, we welcome you to open your brain to the rich embroidery of implications, stories, and convictions that have been joined with the set of all animals. Together, we will disentangle the significant associations among people and creatures, and in doing as such, we desire to acquire a more profound comprehension of the social and otherworldly scenes that have molded the human experience.

In the accompanying parts, we will dive into the universe of creature emblems, investigate creation fantasies including creatures, unravel the imagery of different animals, and look at the job of creatures in customs and functions. We will likewise wander into the domain of old stories and tales, consider the natural and preservation ramifications of creature imagery, and examine the persevering through effect of creatures on contemporary culture. Through this investigation, we plan to uncover the significant and persevering through meaning of creatures in the aggregate human awareness and the assorted manners by which they have advanced our lives and our comprehension of the world.

1. **Definition of Animal Symbolism**

   Creature imagery is a diverse and significant part of human culture that rises above geological, worldly, and social limits. It includes the attribution of emblematic or figurative implications to explicit creatures or gatherings of creatures. This training has continued for centuries, molding the manner in which people see the normal world, their place inside it, and the profound and virtues they hold dear. This investigation digs into the definition, importance, and aspects of creature imagery, revealing insight into the complicated manners by which it has advanced our social, otherworldly, and scholarly scenes.

   Characterizing Creature Imagery

   Creature imagery includes the act of attributing emblematic, figurative, or metaphorical implications to creatures, whether as individual animals or gatherings of related species. These representative implications can be assorted, frequently mirroring the specific social, geological, or verifiable setting in which they are found. While creature imagery is innately emotional and not entirely clear, it assumes an imperative part in human correspondence, narrating, and the transmission of social and otherworldly qualities.

   Social Variety: One of the main traits of creature imagery is its flexibility to different societies and conviction frameworks. Various social orders characteristic different implications to creatures, frequently established in their extraordinary encounters, conditions, and chronicles. For instance, the imagery of the wolf in Local American societies varies from its depiction in European old stories.

   Prototype Characteristics: Creature images are frequently connected with model characteristics and qualities. For example, the lion is much of the time connected with strength and boldness, while the owl is associated with shrewdness and prescience. These prototype characteristics act as all inclusive topics that resound across societies.

   Legendary Importance: Numerous creature images have profound associations with folklore, where they assume focal parts in creation stories, legend excursions, and moral tales. Fanciful creatures, whether genuine or incredible, exemplify complex credits and illustrations.

   Profound and Strict Importance: Different strict and otherworldly practices consolidate creatures as images of divine nature, gatekeepers, or go-betweens between the physical and otherworldly domains. Creatures might be worshipped as divinities or thought about consecrated in specific ceremonies.

   Figurative Language: Creature imagery likewise works as a type of figurative language. In writing and craftsmanship, creatures are utilized to convey complex thoughts and feelings, offering perusers and watchers a rich range of affiliations and implications.

The Unique Idea of Creature Imagery

Creature imagery is certainly not a static idea yet a dynamic and developing one. It adjusts to the significantly impacting requirements and viewpoints of human social orders after some time. As societies connect and develop, so too does the imagery related with creatures. This dynamism is especially clear in the manner that creatures can epitomize both positive and negative characteristics, contingent upon the unique situation.

Positive and Negative Imagery: Numerous creatures are pervaded with dualistic imagery. For example, the snake is frequently connected with both allurement and shrewdness. This duality considers a more nuanced comprehension of the job of creatures in human culture.

Moving Implications: The representative importance of creatures can change as social orders advance and adjust. For instance, the wolf, when a dreaded hunter in European fables, has seen its picture shift to one of jeopardized and safeguarded species as present day protection endeavors have developed.

Social Allotment: As societies interface, they might suitable creature images from each other. These acquired images might obtain new implications and relationship inside the embracing society.

The All inclusiveness of Creature Imagery

While creature imagery can be profoundly well defined for individual societies, it likewise displays noteworthy comprehensiveness. Certain creature images and model characteristics rise above social limits, uncovering the principal associations people share with the normal world and with each other.

Model Creatures: A few creatures, like the hawk or the snake, show up as images in a wide cluster of societies. These animals typify model characteristics like opportunity or change that resound with individuals around the world.

Shared Feelings and Values: Creature imagery frequently takes advantage of general human feelings and values. For instance, creatures related with parenthood, similar to the supporting bear, summon sensations of care and assurance that are diverse.

Shared Fears and Tensions: Creatures that motivate dread, like the wolf or the bug, may likewise hold shared imagery, mirroring mankind's aggregate nerves and difficulties.

Creature Imagery By and by

Creature imagery tracks down articulation in different aspects of human existence, from religion and folklore to writing, workmanship, and ordinary correspondence. It assumes a crucial part in conveying complex thoughts, values, and feelings through a common representative language.

Religion and Otherworldliness: In numerous strict practices, creatures are worshipped as gods or represent divine characteristics. For instance, the cow is sacrosanct in Hinduism, addressing fruitfulness and maternal consideration.

Folklore: Creatures frequently highlight noticeably in the creation legends and stories of various societies. In Norse folklore, the extraordinary world snake Jörmungandr circles the Earth, implying patterns of life and passing.

Legends and Tales: Creature imagery is common in old stories and tales, where creatures act as moral specialists, giving examples and shrewdness. Aesop's tales, highlighting animals like the turtle and the rabbit, outline the getting through force of these accounts.

Workmanship and Writing: Painters, scholars, and different specialists as often as possible utilize creature imagery to convey complex thoughts or feelings. For instance, George Orwell's "Animal Homestead" utilizes human creatures to caricaturize political philosophies and cultural designs.

Language and Sayings: Creature imagery is implanted in regular language and colloquial articulations. Phrases like "smart as a whip" or "difficult as a donkey" utilize creature credits to portray human characteristics.

2. **Importance of Animals in Mythology**

Folklore, as a basic component of human culture, is loaded with stories and images that resound profoundly with the human experience. Creatures, both genuine and envisioned, play had a focal impact in these stories, frequently filling in as characters permeated with significant importance. The significance of creatures in folklore stretches out a long ways past simple narrating; it mirrors mankind's mind boggling relationship with the normal world and uncovers immortal illustrations about the human condition, ethical quality, and otherworldliness. This investigation dives into the complex manners by which creatures have been woven into the texture of legendary practices, revealing insight into their persevering through pertinence and effect on human idea and culture.

The Job of Creatures in Fanciful Stories

Folklore, as the storehouse of social convictions, stories, and strict lessons, has reliably highlighted creatures in different jobs. These animals frequently act as dynamic specialists, encapsulating fundamental characteristics and model credits. They are not simple aloof images but rather unique characters with particular characters, inspirations, and jobs.

Gatekeepers and Defenders: In numerous fanciful practices, creatures are depicted as defenders and watchmen of explicit domains, people, or ideas. For instance, the Hindu goddess Durga is portrayed riding a tiger, representing her power and capacity to beat misfortune.

Creation and Change: Creatures assume a focal part in creation stories, frequently representing the extraordinary force of life and passing. In old Egyptian folklore, the scarab bug addressed the sun's day to day resurrection and the pattern of life.

Moral and Moral Examples: Tales and moral stories, which are a subset of folklore, frequently include creatures as characters that give important illustrations. Aesop's tales, for example, "The Turtle and the Rabbit," utilize creatures to show moral standards.

Images of God and Heavenly Traits: Creatures are every now and again connected with divinities and heavenly characteristics. In Hinduism, the elephant-headed god Ganesha represents astuteness, mind, and the evacuation of snags.

Psychopomps and Delegates: A few creatures are viewed as psychopomps, directing spirits between domains. In Norse folklore, the Valkyries were frequently connected with birds and ponies, accompanying heroes to the hereafter.

The Astronomical Zoological display: Creatures in Creation Fantasies

Creation legends offer a remarkable window into the significance of creatures in folklore. These accounts investigate the beginnings of the world, humankind, and the powers that shape the universe. Creatures every now and again assume key parts in these accounts, addressing essential parts of presence.

World-Framing Monsters: In numerous creation legends, creatures are dynamic members in the arrangement of the world. In Norse folklore, the early stage cow Audumla fed the principal creatures from the ice.

Creature Gods and Creation: A few creatures are themselves viewed as divinities in creation fantasies, with the ability to shape reality. For example, the old Egyptian god Thoth, frequently portrayed as an ibis or primate, assumed a part in making the world and laying out request.

Histories and Creature Prime examples: Creation legends frequently present prototype creatures that act as standards for human way of behaving. The snake in the Nursery of Eden, for instance, exemplifies the dualities of information and allurement.

Allegorical Zoological displays: Creatures as Images

Creatures in folklore likewise capability as images that address many characteristics, feelings, and qualities. These images are much of the time used to pass complex thoughts and on to incite thought, conversation, and reflection.

Temperances and Indecencies: Creatures can represent ideals and indecencies. The lion, frequently depicted as daring and respectable, may address fortitude, while the snake exemplifies duplicity and sly.

Social Variety in Imagery: Various societies might allot particular implications to a similar creature. The owl, for example, is related with astuteness in certain societies and premonition in others.

General Language of Creature Similitudes: Creature representations structure an all inclusive language that rises above social obstructions. They empower the correspondence of intricate ideas through recognizable images, making them open and engaging to different crowds.

Monsters in Divine Pretense: Human Gods

In a few fanciful practices, divine beings and goddesses are portrayed with creature credits, obscuring the limits between the human and creature domains. These human divinities exemplify both human and creature characteristics.

Zoomorphism: Zoomorphism is the act of crediting creature attributes to divine beings and goddesses. For instance, the Hindu god Vishnu is frequently portrayed with the top of a lion.

Divine Shapeshifters: A gods can shapeshift into creature structures. In Greek folklore, Zeus changed into a swan to entice Leda.

Half and half Creatures: Crossover divinities that consolidate human and creature highlights are normal in folklores around the world. The old Egyptian god Anubis had the top of a jackal, filling in as a manual for eternity.

Creatures in Customs and Functions

Fanciful creatures are not restricted to stories and images; they likewise assume a critical part in customs and services. These animals are summoned in strict practices to work with correspondence with the heavenly and to convey significant social qualities.

Conciliatory Creatures and Formal Practices: Creatures are forfeited in different strict customs to assuage divine beings, guarantee richness, or imprint critical life altering situations. This training mirrors a perplexing interchange of imagery and custom.

Creature Celebrations and Festivities: Many societies have celebrations and festivities that unmistakably include creatures. These occasions frequently recognize social legacy, offer thanks for nature's abundance, or conjure divine endowments.

The Job of Creatures in Divination: Certain creatures are related with divination works on, going about as delegates between the human and profound domains. For instance, the perception of birds' flight designs or the guts of conciliatory creatures was utilized in divination in antiquated Rome.

Legends and Tales: Creature Stories and Ethical quality Stories

Creature folklore stretches out past strict and profound settings, tracking down articulation in old stories and tales. These accounts, frequently including human creatures, convey moral and moral examples.

Aesop's Tales and Creature Profound quality: Aesop's tales, an assortment of brief tales, use creatures as characters to bestow moral illustrations. "The Fox and the Grapes" shows the idea of jealousy, while "The Turtle and the Rabbit" highlights the worth of determination.

Monster Legends in World Writing: Monster stories, story sonnets highlighting creatures as characters, have been key to world writing. The epic of "Reynard the Fox" in European writing, for example, utilizes creature characters to investigate complex subjects of ethical quality and society.

Examples from Creature Stories: Creature accounts in fables act as mirrors reflecting human ways of behaving, values, and the outcomes of our activities. They energize self-reflection and proposition direction on the most proficient method to explore the difficulties of life.

Fantasies, Nature, and Protection

Fanciful creatures and their accounts likewise converge with contemporary natural and preservation issues. Native insight and antiquated folklores contain significant experiences into humankind's relationship with the regular world.

Native Insight and Natural Morals: Native societies frequently hold profound biological information and moral points of view that underscore the interconnectedness of every single living being. The accounts of the Haida public and their relationship with the raven, for instance, uncover significant natural bits of knowledge.

Creatures in Current Environment and Preservation Developments: Present day natural and protection developments draw motivation from folklore and native convictions. Endeavors to safeguard imperiled species and protect environments frequently summon creature imagery to bring issues to light and rouse activity.

Pertinence of Creature Folklore in Ecological Issues: The illustrations of creature folklore keep on resounding in contemporary ecological talk, empowering a more amicable relationship with the regular world and advancing mindful stewardship of the climate.

3. **Purpose and Scope of the Book**

"Monsters and Convictions: Creature Imagery and Folklore Across Societies" is an extensive investigation of the rich and unpredictable universe of creature imagery and folklore. This book is driven by the conviction that the connection among people and creatures goes past simple actual conjunction; it stretches out into the domain of imagery, fantasy, and significant social importance. The motivation behind this section is to clarify the overall objectives of the book and characterize its extension, making way for a significant excursion through the intricate embroidery of human-creature connections across time, geology, and culture.

The Complex Motivation behind the Book

This book fills a few significant needs, every one of which adds to a more profound comprehension of creature imagery and folklore in human culture:

Investigation and Documentation: The main role is to investigate and record the different manners by which creatures have been coordinated into the other-worldly, social, and fanciful scenes of different social orders. By inspecting the stories, images, and customs connected with creatures, we intend to give an exhaustive perspective on the multi-layered job they play.

Social Trade: The book looks to advance social trade and appreciation. By digging into the legends and imagery of various societies, we try to cultivate a more profound regard for the variety of human points of view on creatures and nature.

Prototype Bits of knowledge: The investigation of creature imagery frequently uncovers general models and subjects that reverberate across societies. Investigating these common images and characteristics can reveal insight into the consistent ideas that tight spot humankind's relationship with the normal world.

Biological and Preservation Mindfulness: A hidden motivation behind the book is to cause to notice the significance of creature imagery in contemporary environmental and protection issues. We expect to feature the bits of knowledge and shrewdness implanted in old legends that can illuminate present-day ecological morals and backing.

Scholarly Investigation: The book welcomes perusers to participate in scholarly investigation, empowering them to ponder the profound imagery encompassing creatures in folklore and its suggestions for human comprehension of the world.

The Extensive Extent of the Book

"Monsters and Convictions" includes a wide and various scope of points, investigating creature imagery and folklore across a huge number of societies, verifiable periods, and disciplines. The book's extension is organized to give an intensive assessment of this multi-layered subject:

Social Variety: The book investigates creature imagery and folklore across different societies, including however not restricted to antiquated Egyptian, Local American, Norse, Hindu, African, and Greco-Roman practices. Every part dives into the extraordinary viewpoints and stories that various societies have woven around creatures.

Authentic Point of view: The degree stretches out across time, venturing into old, middle age, and contemporary periods. By looking at the advancement of creature imagery over the long run, we expect to explain the powerful idea of this relationship.

Folklore and Religion: The book dives into the jobs of creatures in folklore and religion, looking at their importance as gods, original characters, and mediators between the physical and profound domains.

Legends and Tales: Fables and tales from different societies give understanding into the moral and moral illustrations implanted in creature stories. These stories engage as well as confer ageless insight.

Workmanship, Writing, and Mainstream society: "Monsters and Convictions" investigates the tradition of creature imagery in imaginative articulation, writing, and contemporary mainstream society. It uncovers how creatures proceed to move and impact human innovativeness and creative mind.

Natural and Preservation Pertinence: The book explores the biological and protection ramifications of creature imagery. Drawing from native insight and antiquated folklores, it accentuates the examples implanted in these convictions for tending to present day ecological difficulties.

Interdisciplinary Methodology: "Monsters and Convictions" embraces an interdisciplinary methodology that integrates humanities, relative religion, social examinations, fables, and ecological investigations. This approach considers an exhaustive assessment of the topic.

4. **Methodology and Approach**

The investigation of creature imagery and folklore is a perplexing and complex undertaking that requires an organized strategy and a multidisciplinary approach. "Monsters and Convictions: Creature Imagery and Folklore Across Societies" looks to investigate the significant universe of human-creature connections in different social and verifiable settings completely. This section clarifies the procedure directing our investigation and the methodology utilized to give an all encompassing comprehension of the topic.

Strategic Establishments

The strategy took on in this book is grounded in sound examination standards and draws from a different scope of sources and teaches. It is based upon the accompanying key strategic establishments:

Interdisciplinary Methodology: The investigation of creature imagery and folklore is innately interdisciplinary, drawing from fields like humanities, relative religion, social examinations, fables, and ecological investigations. This approach takes into consideration an exhaustive assessment of the topic by considering different social, verifiable, and biological points of view.

Social Responsiveness: A focal systemic principle of this study is social responsiveness. Moving toward creature imagery and folklore with deference for the convictions and customs of different cultures is fundamental. This involves a promise to understanding the setting inside which creatures are represented and worshipped in various social orders.

Near Examination: To explain the widespread subjects and varieties in creature imagery and folklore, a relative examination is utilized. This approach includes analyzing comparative subjects or creatures across different societies and recognizing shared characteristics and contrasts in their representative implications.

Multisource Exploration: This procedure depends on a great many sources, including old texts, oral practices, strict sacred writings, old stories, scholastic examination, and contemporary records. By drawing from various sources, we plan to give a nuanced and complete point of view regarding the matter.

Social and Worldly Setting: The social and transient setting inside which creatures are represented and mythologized is basic. This system considers the verifiable and sociocultural foundations of every practice to figure out the unique idea of creature imagery over the long haul.

Ethnographic Examinations: Ethnographic investigations, which include first-hand perceptions and meetings with people from assorted social foundations, are utilized to acquire bits of knowledge into the living customs of creature imagery and folklore in contemporary settings.

Way to deal with Investigating Creature Imagery and Folklore

The way to deal with investigating creature imagery and folklore is a diverse and organized one, including the accompanying key aspects:

Social and Geographic Variety: The book is coordinated around the investigation of creature imagery and folklore in different societies and geological areas. Every part is committed to a particular social or provincial setting, giving a nitty gritty assessment of the novel convictions, stories, and imagery encompassing creatures.

Verifiable Assessment: To comprehend the advancement of creature imagery, every section dives into the authentic setting of the way of life viable. This approach takes into account the assessment of how imagery and folklore have advanced over the long haul.

Strict and Otherworldly Importance: Creatures frequently assume focal parts in strict and profound practices. The book investigates the meaning of creatures as gods, delegates, and images of heavenliness in different conviction frameworks, revealing insight into their profound and moral implications.

Legends and Tales: Old stories and tales highlighting creatures as characters are analyzed to reveal the moral and moral illustrations implanted in these accounts. The book expects to feature the job of creatures as moral specialists and narrators.

Imaginative Articulation: The tradition of creature imagery in workmanship and writing is investigated to comprehend how creatures keep on motivating human innovativeness and articulation. The book breaks down how craftsmen and journalists utilize creature imagery to convey complex thoughts and feelings.

Natural and Preservation Suggestions: "Monsters and Convictions" explores the biological and protection significance of creature imagery and folklore. By drawing from native insight and old convictions, the book stresses the examples implanted in these customs for tending to contemporary natural difficulties.

Contextual analyses and Models: The book consolidates contextual analyses and models from different societies and authentic periods to represent the variety and intricacy of creature imagery and folklore. These genuine models improve the story and give a more complete comprehension of the subject.

Similar and Logical System

One of the focal parts of the methodology in "Monsters and Convictions" is a similar and scientific system. Every section investigates the imagery and folklore of explicit creatures or subjects across societies, empowering perusers to distinguish consistent ideas and particular translations. This approach works with a more profound enthusiasm for both the comprehensiveness and social variety of creature imagery and folklore.

Besides, the logical system is utilized to look at the moral, moral, and environmental components of creature imagery and folklore. By fundamentally evaluating the job of creatures in these unique situations, the book expects to reveal insight into the persevering through significance and effect of these convictions on contemporary issues.

Chapter 1

The Significance of Animals in Human Culture

From the earliest long stretches of human life, creatures have assumed a significant and complex part in human culture. They have filled in as wellsprings of food, friendship, images, and wellsprings of motivation. The connection among people and creatures is profoundly interwoven, and it essentially affects the advancement of human culture over the entire course of time. This paper investigates the different manners by which creatures have affected and improved human culture, from ancient times to the advanced period.

1. **Creatures as a Wellspring of Food**

   Quite possibly of the most essential manner by which creatures have formed human culture is through their job as a wellspring of food. For quite a bit of mankind's set of experiences, hunting and assembling were the essential method for endurance, and creatures gave a urgent wellspring of food, dress, and devices. Early people depended on their insight into the way of behaving and propensities for creatures to chase and trap them really.

   The training of creatures denoted a critical crossroads in mankind's set of experiences, considering the change from traveling, agrarian ways of life to settled horticultural networks. Animals like cows, sheep, and goats were among quick to be trained, giving meat and dairy as well as work for cultivating. This change in way of life brought about the improvement of civic establishments and the foundation of culture as language, religion, and craftsmanship.

   Creatures have likewise assumed a huge part in the improvement of food all over the planet. Various societies have fostered their own culinary practices in light of the creatures accessible to them. For instance, hamburger is fundamental to the food of numerous Western societies, while in India, the cow is thought of as holy and isn't devoured. In Japan, sushi and sashimi highlight different marine creatures, mirroring the significance of fish in Japanese culture.

2. **Creatures as Partners**

Past their utilitarian worth, creatures have additionally been appreciated as side-kicks by people for centuries. The connection among people and creatures as pets is a demonstration of the close to home and mental advantages that creatures give. Canines, felines, and ponies, among others, play played focal parts in human homes and hearts.

Canines, frequently alluded to as "man's closest companion," have been reared for different purposes, from hunting to monitoring and friendship. Their faithfulness and warmth have made them adored individuals from innumerable families. Felines, as well, have had a long history of friendship with people, offering nuisance control and charming themselves to their human partners with their energetic and free nature.

Ponies, then again, have been both working creatures and loyal colleagues. They have filled in as transportation, helped with agribusiness, and assumed crucial parts in fighting over the entire course of time. Their polish, strength, and devotion have prompted profound associations among people and these superb animals.

Past the more normal pets, different creatures, like birds, reptiles, and fascinating creatures, have additionally been kept as colleagues in various societies all over the planet. The connections framed with these creatures mirror the different manners by which creatures advance living souls.

3. **Creatures as Images and Legends**

Creatures have filled in as images and themes in human culture, folklore, and religion however long these features of human life have existed. In many societies, creatures are pervaded with emblematic implications and frequently address unique ideas, values, or divinities.

In old Egyptian culture, for example, the feline was related with the goddess Bastet, who addressed home, fruitfulness, and labor. In Hinduism, the cow is worshipped as an image of parenthood and is viewed as consecrated. In Local American societies, the falcon is an image of solidarity and otherworldliness.

Creatures additionally highlight noticeably in legends and old stories. The Greek fantasy of the Minotaur, for instance, is based on an animal with the body of a man and the top of a bull. The Chinese zodiac, with its twelve creature signs, is a conspicuous piece of Chinese culture, impacting parts of day to day existence, including horoscopes and fortune-telling.

Creatures have likewise been utilized to pass moral illustrations and social qualities on through tales and stories. Aesop's tales, for example, frequently highlight creatures as characters, with stories that grant intelligence and show life illustrations.

4. **Creatures in Craftsmanship and Writing**

Creatures have been a continuous subject in artistic expression, filling in as motivation for canvases, figures, writing, and different types of imaginative articulation. Over the entire course of time, specialists have portrayed creatures in different styles and settings to convey their excellence, imagery, or the human-creature association.

In the realm of visual expressions, creatures have been a well known subject for painters and stone carvers. Leonardo da Vinci's "Vitruvian Man" is a notable illustration of how creatures, for this situation, the circle and square, have been utilized to investigate the connection among people and the regular world. Untamed life craftsmanship, similar to crafted by John James Audubon, praises the excellence and variety of creature life.

Writing, as well, is loaded with creature imagery and subjects. George Orwell's "Animal Homestead" is a figurative novella that utilizes a gathering of livestock to caricaturize political and get-togethers. Aesop's tales, as referenced prior, use creatures to convey moral examples. In youngsters' writing, creatures frequently assume focal parts in stories and stories, cultivating sympathy and showing significant qualities.

5. **Creatures in Religion and Custom**

   Religion and custom have frequently integrated creatures into their practices and convictions. In numerous old and contemporary strict practices, creatures hold a hallowed or representative importance.

   In Hinduism, the cow is loved as a hallowed creature and represents parenthood, sustenance, and immaculateness. The cow's significance is to such an extent that it is frequently treated with profound regard and thought about an image of the heavenly. In old Egypt, creatures like felines, ibises, and crocodiles were related with different gods and assumed a focal part in strict ceremonies.

   Creatures have likewise been forfeited in strict functions for of expiation, conciliation, or offering. In old times, different societies rehearsed creature penance, trusting it to be an approach to speaking with the heavenly. In contemporary religions, for example, Islam and Judaism, creature penance is as yet performed during explicit strict celebrations.

   The emblematic utilization of creatures in strict iconography and folklore can likewise be found in Christianity, where the sheep is an image of guiltlessness and immaculateness, and the pigeon addresses the Essence of God. In Buddhism, the lotus bloom, frequently connected with immaculateness, edification, and resurrection, is some of the time portrayed with a couple of brilliant fish swimming underneath it.

6. **Protection and Ecological Mindfulness**

   As human social orders have created and extended, the connection among people and creatures has developed. With expanding urbanization and industrialization, people have become more detached from the normal world and the creatures that possess it. Nonetheless, this partition has likewise led to a developing familiarity with the significance of preservation and ecological insurance.

The investigation of creatures and their biological systems has turned into a critical field of logical request. Preservation endeavors intend to safeguard imperiled species, save biodiversity, and keep up with the fragile equilibrium of environments. Ecological associations and drives work to bring issues to light of the effect of human exercises in the world and advance supportable practices.

Creatures have become images of the ecological development. Symbols like the polar bear, whose territory is undermined by environmental change, or the elephant, whose ivory exchange has prompted populace declines, definitely stand out to squeezing ecological issues. Activists and associations utilize these images to accumulate support for preservation endeavors and push for strategy changes.

7. **Creatures in Mainstream society**

Creatures have made a permanent imprint on mainstream society, forming the manner in which individuals engage themselves and collaborate with their general surroundings. From youth toys to blockbuster films, creatures have a huge presence in current diversion.

Youngsters' writing and enlivened films frequently include creatures as primary characters. Works of art like "The Wilderness Book" and "Winnie the Pooh" have spellbound ages of youthful perusers and watchers. These accounts offer diversion as well as moral examples, advancing qualities like companionship, consideration, and mental fortitude.

In the realm of sports, animals have roused group names and mascots, adding to the personality of sports groups and establishments. The Chicago Bulls, the Atlanta Falcons, and the Toronto Raptors are only a couple of instances of pro athletics groups named after creatures. Mascots like the San Diego Chicken and the Phillie Phanatic have become cherished images of their particular groups.

Creatures likewise assume an unmistakable part in the film and broadcast business. From Disney's "The Lion Lord" to "Tracking down Nemo" and "Jurassic Park," creatures have been key to probably the best and esteemed motion pictures in realistic history. They have the ability to bring out a large number of feelings and interface with crowds on a profound level.

8. **The Moral and Moral Components of Human-Creature Connections**

While creatures have been necessary to human culture, their treatment and use have brought up moral and moral issues. The abuse of creatures for food, clothing, and logical exploration has prompted banters about basic entitlements and government assistance.

The basic entitlements development advocates for the moral treatment of creatures, contending that they have inherent worth and ought not be exposed to superfluous damage and languishing. Savants and activists like Peter Artist have contended that creatures have interests and ought to be viewed as in moral navigation.

Issues, for example, production line cultivating, creature testing, and the fur and ivory exchanges have gone under examination. Creature government assistance regulations and guidelines have been carried out in different nations to address worries about the treatment of creatures in different enterprises. This has prompted changes in rehearses, like the push toward more compassionate cultivating and research facility techniques.

The connection among people and creatures additionally brings up issues about the ethical obligation of people as stewards of the planet. Ecological morals, which investigates the moral elements of human collaborations with the normal world, has become progressively applicable as human exercises have prompted environment annihilation, species elimination, and environmental change.

1.1 Historical Overview

A verifiable outline gives a fundamental structure to grasping the development of human social orders, civic establishments, and the world overall. This paper plans to give a compact verifiable outline, crossing from the earliest recorded mankind's set of experiences to the current day, featuring key occasions, improvements, and defining moments that have molded our reality. While it is difficult to cover each huge occasion exhaustively, this outline will address significant periods and achievements, assisting with drawing an obvious conclusion of mankind's set of experiences.

1. **Ancient Times**

   Mankind's set of experiences starts in ancient times, a long time before the development of composing. In this time, our progenitors lived as tracker finders, depending on scavenging and chasing after food. Over the long run, people created instruments and found farming, which denoted a critical shift toward settled social orders. The Neolithic Upset, around 10,000 BCE, saw the improvement of horticulture and the foundation of the main rural networks. As people cultivated and tame creatures, they made surplus food, prompting populace development and the rise of early civic establishments.

2. **Antiquated Developments**

   The time of old developments is described by the ascent of mind boggling social orders with cutting edge societies, states, and composed dialects. The absolute most noticeable antiquated developments include:

   Mesopotamia: In the district between the Tigris and Euphrates streams, the Sumerians, Akkadians, Babylonians, and Assyrians constructed progressed city-states with frameworks of composing, regulation, and math.

   Egypt: Along the Nile Stream, the old Egyptians fostered an exceptionally coordinated society, with surprising accomplishments in design (pyramids), hieroglyphic composition, and a rich strict custom.

Indus Valley: In what is presently cutting edge Pakistan and northwest India, the Indus Valley Development thrived, with noteworthy metropolitan preparation, waste frameworks, and a content that stays undeciphered.

China: Old China saw the rise of traditions like the Shang, Zhou, and Qin, known for their philosophical commitments (Confucianism and Daoism) and innovations like paper, printing, and black powder.

Greece: Antiquated Greece delivered powerful logicians (Socrates, Plato, Aristotle), laid out equitable administration, and established the groundwork for Western way of thinking, science, and writing.

Rome: The Roman Republic and Domain significantly affected the Western world, with achievements in regulation, designing, and administration. The spread of Christianity during this period additionally molded the course of history.

3. **Medieval times**

   The Medieval times, otherwise called the archaic period, spread over generally from the fifth to the fifteenth century CE. This period was set apart by the predominance of feudalism, the force of the Catholic Church, and huge political and social turns of events. Striking occasions and peculiarities during the Medieval times include:

   The Byzantine Realm: The Eastern Roman Domain, focused in Byzantium (later Constantinople, presently Istanbul), safeguarded and sent old style information while fostering its extraordinary social personality.

   The Islamic Brilliant Age: The Islamic world made huge advances in science, arithmetic, medication, and reasoning, with researchers like Ibn Sina (Avicenna) and Ibn Rushd (Averroes) adding to human information.

   The Campaigns: A progression of strict conflicts among Christians and Muslims over control of the Sacred Land, which lastingly affected European culture and the connection between the East and West.

   The Renaissance: A social and scholarly development that arose in Italy during the late Medieval times and denoted a restoration of interest in workmanship, writing, and gaining from old style relic.

4. **Early Present day Period**

   The early present day period, which ranges from the late fifteenth to the late eighteenth 100 years, saw a progression of extraordinary occasions and improvements that established the groundwork for the cutting edge world:

   The Period of Investigation: European pilgrims, similar to Christopher Columbus, Vasco da Gama, and Ferdinand Magellan, set out on ventures that extended the well explored regions of the planet, prompting the trading of merchandise, societies, and thoughts in the Columbian Trade.

   The Protestant Renewal: Started by Martin Luther in 1517, this strict development tested the power of the Roman Catholic Church and prompted the foundation of different Protestant divisions.

The Edification: A time of scholarly and philosophical development that underlined reason, independence, and doubt of conventional power, cultivating progressions in science, governmental issues, and common liberties.

The Logical Transformation: Spearheaded by figures like Galileo Galilei and Isaac Newton, this period denoted a shift from strict clarifications of the normal world to observational, logical request.

The Period of Unrests: The late eighteenth century saw a progression of political disturbances, including the American Transformation, the French Insurgency, and the Haitian Upset, that laid the preparation for present day ideas of a majority rules government and common freedoms.

5. **The Modern Upheaval and Modernization**

The Modern Upheaval, which started in the late eighteenth hundred years in England and spread across Europe and the US, denoted a significant change in mankind's set of experiences. It was portrayed by the automation of creation, urbanization, and quick mechanical progressions, including the steam motor, material hardware, and the expansion of production lines.

This period prompted huge cultural changes, including the ascent of the common laborers, the development of urban areas, and changes in financial and social designs. The development of industry and business worked with expansionism and dominion, as Western powers tried to apply impact and command over different regions of the planet.

6. **nineteenth and twentieth Hundreds of years**

The nineteenth century saw a continuation of the Modern Upheaval and critical political turns of events:

The American Nationwide conflict: A contention from 1861 to 1865 that brought about the cancelation of subjugation in the US and the protection of the Association.

European Government: European powers extended their frontier domains in Asia and Africa, molding worldwide legislative issues, exchange, and culture.

The Scramble for Africa: The late nineteenth century saw a race among European powers to guarantee an area in Africa, bringing about the frontier division of the landmass.

The twentieth century was set apart by two universal conflicts, significant political and social changes, and the beginning of the advanced mechanical age:

The Second Great War: A worldwide struggle from 1914 to 1918 that had wrecking outcomes and reshaped the international scene.

The Russian Upheaval: In 1917, the Trotskyites, drove by Vladimir Lenin, toppled the Russian Temporary Government and laid out a socialist state.

The Economic crisis of the early 20s: A serious overall monetary decline during the 1930s that prompted social and political disturbance.

The Second Great War: One more worldwide clash from 1939 to 1945, which had a significantly more prominent effect than The Second Great War, bringing about the production of the Assembled Countries and the division of the world into the Eastern and Western coalitions during the Virus War.

The Virus War: A drawn out philosophical struggle between the US and the Soviet Association, described by an atomic weapons contest and intermediary wars.

The Social equality Development: A social and political development in the US that tried to end racial isolation and segregation.

The Space Race: A contest between the US and the Soviet Association to accomplish achievements in space investigation.

7. **The Contemporary Time**

The last option part of the twentieth 100 years and the mid 21st century have seen huge turns of events, including:

The finish of the Virus War: The breakdown of the Soviet Association in 1991 denoted the finish of the bipolar world request and the rise of the US as the sole superpower.

Innovative Progressions: The computerized unrest, the ascent of the web, and the multiplication of cell phones have changed the manner in which individuals impart, work, and live.

Globalization: The interconnectedness of economies, societies, and social orders has prompted expanded worldwide exchange, social trade, and the spread of thoughts.

Environmental Change and Ecological Worries: The acknowledgment of environmental change as a squeezing worldwide issue has prompted peaceful accords and endeavors to battle its belongings.

Illegal intimidation and Security: The occasions of September 11, 2001, and resulting worldwide fear based oppressor assaults essentially affect global security and legislative issues.

The Bedouin Spring: A progression of uprisings and fights across the Center East and North Africa in 2010-2011, bringing about changes in initiative and continuous contentions.

Progresses in Medication and Wellbeing: Advancements in medical care, like genomics and the improvement of antibodies, have worked on human wellbeing and expanded future.

1.2 Psychological and Cultural Significance

The exchange among brain science and culture is an intricate and multi-layered peculiarity that shapes the manner in which people see, comprehend, and cooperate with their general surroundings. Culture, characterized as the common convictions, values, standards, and practices of a gathering, applies a significant effect on the mental turn of events and working of people. This article investigates the mental and social meaning of this powerful relationship, inspecting what culture means for human way of behaving, perception, feelings, personality, and psychological well-being.

1. **Social Impacts on Discernment and Insight**

   Culture altogether impacts how people see and decipher the world. The manner in which we see, hear, and figure out our environmental elements still up in the air by our science but on the other hand is formed by the social setting in which we are raised. Central issues to consider include:

   Language and Thought: Language is an essential part of culture, and the construction of a language can impact how people think and reason. Various dialects have differing phonetic classifications and ideas, which can influence mental cycles. For instance, a few societies have words or articulations for ideas that are absent in different dialects.

   Perceptual Contrasts: Social varieties in discernment can appear in visual and hear-able spaces. For example, a few societies might put more accentuation on specific tones, prompting contrasts in variety discernment. Social varieties in melodic inclinations and apparent responsiveness likewise reflect how discernment is molded by social standards.

   Social Systems: Social patterns and mental structures shape how people decipher occasions and encounters. These systems incorporate social contents, generalizations, and assumptions that guide conduct and impact the translation of expressive gestures.

2. **Culture and Social Way of behaving**

   Culture assumes a urgent part in shaping social way of behaving and cooperations. Social standards and values direct the way that people connect with each other, impart, and structure social bonds. Key parts of social importance in friendly way of behaving include:

   Correspondence Styles: Various societies have unmistakable correspondence styles, including direct versus aberrant correspondence, high-setting versus low-setting correspondence, and the utilization of nonverbal prompts. These distinctions influence how people express feelings, make demands, and haggle in friendly circumstances.

   Standards and Decorum: Social standards characterize suitable social way of behaving, including habits, civility, and OK direct out in the open and confidential settings. Penetrating these standards can prompt social outcomes and may bring about people being segregated or underestimated.

   Social Ordered progression: Many societies have laid out progressive systems that direct economic wellbeing and power elements. These ordered progressions impact how people cooperate with each other and the jobs they accept in the public arena. Understanding one's spot in the social ordered progression is critical for exploring social connections.

3. **Culture and Profound Articulation**

Feelings are widespread human encounters, however how they are communicated and perceived can differ across societies. Social importance in close to home articulation incorporates:

Show Rules: Social standards and values direct when and how feelings ought to be communicated. For instance, a few societies support the open articulation of feelings, while others underscore close to home restriction and poise.

Close to home Discernment: Social foundations impact how people see and decipher feelings in others. Diverse examinations have shown varieties in feeling acknowledgment exactness and the significance of setting in deciphering close to home articulations.

Profound Guideline: Social standards likewise influence how people manage their feelings. Societies might have unmistakable strategies for dealing with especially difficult times and customs to deal with close to home pain. For example, reflection and care rehearses in a few Eastern societies are established in close to home guideline and prosperity.

4. **Social Character and Self-Idea**

Culture assumes a fundamental part in molding a singular's self-appreciation and character. Social importance in character advancement incorporates:

Social Character: Social personality includes the parts of a singular's self-idea that are connected with their social foundation. It incorporates angles like identity, ethnicity, religion, and legacy. Social personality is an essential part of a singular's general self-character.

Biculturalism and Multiculturalism: In an undeniably interconnected world, numerous people have bicultural or multicultural personalities. Dealing with the intricacies of numerous social characters can impact confidence, self-idea, and mental prosperity.

Assimilation: Assimilation is the interaction by which people adjust to and embrace the social practices and standards of another culture. Assimilation can prompt changes in a singular's self-idea, as they coordinate parts of the new culture into their character.

5. **Social Importance in Psychological wellness**

Culture altogether influences emotional wellness, affecting how people insight, express, and look for help for mental pain. Understanding social importance in psychological well-being is fundamental for giving viable and socially delicate consideration. Key contemplations include:

Social Conditions: A few societies have exceptional articulations of mental misery known as social disorders. These conditions may not fit conveniently into Western indicative classifications and require a socially educated way to deal with evaluation and treatment.

Disgrace and Help-Chasing: Social standards encompassing psychological well-being and help-chasing can change generally. A few societies might disparage psychological instability, making it challenging for people to look for help. Understanding these social mentalities is significant for offering help.

Social Ability: Psychological well-being experts should foster social skill to work really with people from different foundations. This incorporates figuring out social standards, values, and convictions and adjusting restorative methodologies likewise.

6. **Social Variation and Globalization**

In an undeniably globalized world, the mental and social meaning of variation is especially significant. People and networks should explore the difficulties and chances of social variation. Key contemplations include:

Acculturative Pressure: Adjusting to another culture can distressing and challenge. Acculturative pressure might appear as nervousness, discouragement, or other mental side effects. Emotionally supportive networks and techniques for dealing with this pressure are fundamental.

Worldwide Citizenship: A few people embrace a worldwide citizenship character, rising above public or social limits. Worldwide citizenship underscores shared human qualities and a feeling of obligation for tending to worldwide difficulties.

Social Trade and Hybridity: Globalization has prompted expanded social trade, bringing about cross breed personalities and societies. These arising characters challenge conventional ideas of social importance and personality.

1.3 Animals in Prehistoric Art and Religion

The connection between ancient people and creatures was profoundly interlaced with their endurance, culture, and otherworldliness. Ancient craftsmanship and religion give important experiences into the meaning of creatures in the existences of our far off precursors. These early portrayals of creatures in craftsmanship and strict practices offer a brief look into the human-creature association that existed during the Paleolithic, Neolithic, and other ancient periods. This exposition investigates the job of creatures in ancient workmanship and religion, revealing insight into their social and profound importance.

1. **Ancient Workmanship: The Cavern Canvases**

Paleolithic Workmanship

One of the most notorious and getting through types of ancient workmanship is the cavern compositions that date back huge number of years. These artistic creations, frequently found profound inside caverns and rock covers, uncover the significance of creatures in the otherworldly and social existence of early people.

1. **Chauvet Cavern:** The Chauvet Cavern in France contains the absolute most seasoned known cave canvases, going back around 30,000 to 32,000 years. These complicated and all around saved artworks portray different creatures, including ponies, mammoths, and rhinoceroses. The accuracy and scrupulousness in these craftsmanships recommend a significant veneration for the portrayed creatures.
2. **Lascaux Cavern:** The Lascaux Cavern, additionally in France, contains a striking assortment of Paleolithic cavern workmanship, including portrayals of creatures like aurochs, buffalo, and ponies. These works of art, assessed to be around 17,000 years of age, give experiences into the profound and potentially shamanistic acts of the time.

Neolithic Workmanship

As humankind progressed from agrarian social orders to settled horticultural networks during the Neolithic time frame, the job of creatures in workmanship developed to mirror the changing lifestyle.

1. **Catalhöyük:** The old settlement of Catalhöyük in advanced Turkey, possessed from around 7500 BCE to 5700 BCE, highlights wall paintings and figures that portray creatures. These craftsmanships propose a profound association between the Neolithic public and the creatures they lived close by.
2. **Stonehenge:** The renowned Stonehenge landmark in Britain, developed during the Neolithic time frame, is related with the solstices and equinoxes. While it isn't shrouded in craftsmanship, the meaning of the stones' arrangements to divine occasions shows the connection between the universe, nature, and human otherworldliness.

II. Creatures in Ancient Religion

Ancient religion, frequently alluded to as animism, was well established in the conviction that normal components, including creatures, had otherworldly importance. Creatures assumed a focal part in these early strict practices.

Totemism

Totemism is a strict conviction framework wherein creatures, plants, or other regular components are viewed as the progenitors, defenders, or directing spirits of a specific group or clan. These tribal creatures hold representative and otherworldly importance and frequently act as a wellspring of character for the gathering. Totemism was normal among numerous native societies, particularly those in North America and Australia.

1. **Local American Totemism:** Native clans in North America had complex tribal frameworks in which creatures were worshipped and considered as guides and

defenders. Various clans had their own symbol creatures, which were accepted to exemplify the attributes and powers of the creature being referred to.

2. **Australian Native Symbols:** Native Australians rehearsed totemism, partner explicit creatures and regular components with their familial stories and social character. These emblems were fundamental to their otherworldliness and gave an association with the land and its animals.

Shamanism

Shamanism, a common type of ancient otherworldliness, involved people known as shamans who were accepted to can speak with the soul world. In shamanic rehearses, creatures frequently assumed a crucial part as soul guides, go-betweens, or wellsprings of force.

1. **Cave Workmanship and Shamanism:** A few specialists propose that the ancient cavern compositions might be connected to shamanic ceremonies. The complex portrayals of creatures might have been essential for visionary encounters or customs in which shamans tried to associate with creature spirits for direction and power.

2. **Creature Veils and Customs:** In different ancient societies, the wearing of creature covers during strict functions was a typical practice. These veils represented the change into the soul of the creature, permitting the wearer to encapsulate its qualities and powers.

III. Imagery and Folklore

Ancient societies frequently created folklores that integrated creatures as focal figures. These fantasies were gone down through oral practices and at times portrayed in workmanship, uncovering the persevering through social and emblematic meaning of creatures.

The Incomparable Goddess and the Bull

In old societies like those of Mesopotamia, the love of an Extraordinary Goddess frequently highlighted creatures as images of fruitfulness and power. The bull, specifically, held extraordinary significance in these social orders and was frequently connected with the goddess.

1. **Inanna and Dumuzid:** In Sumerian folklore, Inanna (Ishtar) was the goddess of adoration, richness, and war. She was frequently portrayed with lions, which addressed her power and fierceness. Inanna's sweetheart, Dumuzid, was related with the bull, representing strength and ripeness. The legend of their association and Dumuzid's drop into the hidden world mirrors the repetitive idea of life, passing, and resurrection.

Creature Headed Divinities

In old Egypt, creature headed divinities were a typical element of the strict pantheon. These gods typified both human and creature qualities, mirroring a combination of human and creature imagery.

1. **Ra and the Bird of prey:** Ra, the sun god, was frequently portrayed with the top of a hawk. The hawk addressed his association with the sky and the sun's day to day venture across the sky.
2. **Anubis and the Jackal:** Anubis, the lord of eternity, had the top of a jackal. Jackals were related with graveyards and rummaging, making Anubis a watchman of the dead.

Creature Imagery in Different Societies

Creature imagery reached out to different societies, like antiquated Greece, where the owl was related with Athena, the goddess of intelligence, and the phoenix represented resurrection. In Chinese culture, the mythical beast and the phoenix held extraordinary emblematic importance, addressing majestic power and favorability, separately.

IV. Custom Penance and Creature Contributions

Numerous ancient societies participated in ceremonial practices that elaborate the penance of creatures as contributions to mollify gods or spirits. These ceremonies were accepted to keep up with the equilibrium of the normal world and guarantee the prosperity of the local area.

Old Mesoamerica

In Mesoamerican societies like the Aztecs and the Maya, custom creature penance was a fundamental piece of strict functions. The contribution of creatures, frequently joined by human penances, was viewed as fundamental for keeping up with the blessing of the divine beings and guaranteeing the ripeness of the land.

Old Greece

In old Greece, the act of creature penance, known as "thysia," was a significant part of strict celebrations. Creatures like sheep, goats, and bulls were proposed to divinities like Zeus and Apollo. The custom represented the correspondence among people and the heavenly.

Contributions in Different Societies

Different other ancient societies all over the planet rehearsed creature penance and contributions for of associating with the profound domain. These contributions were accepted to lay out correspondence with the soul world and to give security, richness, and direction.

V. The Change to Present day Convictions and Practices

As social orders developed and societies changed, the job of creatures in religion likewise different. While a few conventional practices have continued, current convictions and practices will quite often be more withdrawn from the immediate dependence on creature imagery, emblems, and customs. The shift away from ancient types of otherworldliness reflects changes in human social orders, perspectives, and moral contemplations.

Chapter 2

Animals as Totems and Spirits

The meaning of creatures in human societies isn't restricted to their jobs as actual creatures in our reality; they likewise assume a significant profound and representative part as symbols and spirits. Over the entire course of time and across societies, people have venerated, regarded, and looked for association with creatures as images of force, insight, direction, and security. This article investigates the different and complex connections among creatures and people as symbols and spirits, analyzing what they have meant for conviction frameworks, customs, and perspectives.

1. **Grasping Totemism**
   Meaning of Totemism
   Totemism is a conviction framework where people lay out a profound association with a specific creature, plant, or regular component, frequently alluded to as a symbol. These emblems are viewed as hallowed and representative, epitomizing the pith and qualities of the related creature or component. Totemism is tracked down in different native societies all over the planet, and the tribal relationship assumes a focal part in forming convictions, characters, and ceremonies.
   Emblematic Affiliations
   Symbols are related with explicit characteristics or qualities that the creature addresses. These representative affiliations might incorporate strength, shrewdness, security, direction, or different characteristics considered fundamental by the way of life being referred to. The decision of an emblem frequently mirrors the qualities and necessities of a specific local area.
2. **Totemism in Native Societies**

Local American Totemism

Local American societies have a rich practice of totemism, with every clan or tribe taking on their own symbols. These symbols normally address creatures, plants, or other regular components. They act as otherworldly aides, defenders, and wellsprings of personality.

1. **Faction Emblems:** In numerous Local American social orders, families or connection bunches are related with explicit symbols, which are in many cases creatures like the wolf, bear, or hawk. Individuals from a tribe worship and regard their symbol as a piece of their more distant family.
2. **Chain of commands:** The native people groups of the Pacific Northwest, like the Haida and Tlingit, are popular for their command hierarchies, extravagantly cut wooden designs that show the emblems of a tribe or family. These command hierarchies act as a visual portrayal of their tribal convictions and narratives.

Australian Native Emblems

Native Australians additionally practice totemism, interfacing profoundly with the regular world and its animals. Every person, family, or clan has their own tribal affiliations.

1. **Connection and Symbols:** In Native societies, emblems are connected to family relationship frameworks, with every individual having a place with at least one tribal gatherings. These tribal affiliations are vital to their personalities and jobs inside the local area.
2. **Dreamtime Stories:** Tribal convictions are intertwined with Dreamtime stories, which make sense of the formation of the world and the starting points of emblems. These accounts are gone down through ages and are fundamental for social safeguarding.

III. Totemism Past Native Societies

While totemism is generally usually connected with native societies, the idea of emblems and tribal connections reaches out past these networks.

New Age and Ecospirituality

In contemporary profound and New Age developments, totemism has seen as another following. Numerous people try to interface with creature emblems as wellsprings of direction, mending, and self-awareness.

1. **Creature Totemism:** Certain individuals accept that they have individual creature emblems that act as soul guides. These symbols might be uncovered through contemplation, dreams, or shamanic rehearses.
2. **Ecospirituality:** Ecospirituality is a cutting edge development that underscores the otherworldly association among people and the regular world, including

creatures. It empowers veneration for all living things and an acknowledgment of the interconnectedness, everything being equal.

Mainstream society

Creatures as emblems and images have likewise advanced into mainstream society, filling in as wellsprings of motivation and recognizable proof.

1. **Sports Groups:** Many games groups embrace creature mascots and emblems, integrating these images into their marking and characters. These mascots frequently address characteristics like strength, dexterity, or cooperation.
2. **Imagery in Writing and Film:** In writing and film, creatures are as often as possible utilized as images to convey more profound implications or subjects. For instance, the lion in "The Lion Ruler" is an image of boldness and initiative.

IV. Soul Creatures and Guides

The idea of soul creatures and soul guides stretches out past totemism and is pervasive in numerous otherworldly and strict conviction frameworks. These aides are frequently connected with individual profound excursions, self-improvement, and insurance.

Soul Guides in Different Societies

1. **Local American Soul Guides:** Local American societies have confidence in soul creatures or creature directs that give direction and assurance. These aides are looked for through vision missions and different ceremonies.
2. **African Soul Creatures:** In numerous African societies, people accept that they have individual soul creatures that watch over them and guide them. These creatures might be uncovered through dreams or initiatory encounters.

Individual Soul Creatures

In current translations of otherworldliness, people frequently look to find their own soul creatures as wellsprings of direction and knowledge.

1. **Contemplation and Dreams:** Certain individuals recognize their soul creatures through reflection or dream encounters. These creatures are remembered to offer insight and backing on one's life way.
2. **Self-improvement and Strengthening:** Finding one's soul creature is frequently connected with self-improvement, self-revelation, and strengthening. These aides are viewed as wellsprings of solidarity and insurance.

V. Imagery and Creature Emblems

The imagery of creature emblems is multi-layered and fluctuates among societies. A few normal representative affiliations include:

Strength: Creatures like the lion, bear, and elephant are frequently connected with physical and inward strength.

Astuteness: The owl, image of shrewdness, is frequently connected to sharp knowledge and instinct.

Insurance: Animals like the wolf and falcon are viewed as defenders, watching people or networks from hurt.

Change: Creatures like the butterfly, image of change, address self-improvement and change.

Variation: The chameleon, with its capacity to change tone, is an image of versatility.

Richness: The bunny, known for its quick generation, represents ripeness and overflow.

VI. Customs and Services

Symbols and soul creatures assume fundamental parts in different customs and functions inside native and profound networks.

Vision Missions: Numerous native societies, particularly among Local American clans, lead vision journeys to look for their own creature symbols. These journeys include fasting, contemplation, and association with the normal world.

Naming Services: In certain societies, an individual's emblem creature might impact their name, mirroring their novel profound association and characteristics.

Mending and Insurance: Symbols are frequently conjured for recuperating functions and security ceremonies. Shamans and medication individuals might call upon the force of symbol creatures to support their work.

VII. Protection and Biological Importance

The acknowledgment of creatures as symbols and spirits additionally conveys biological and preservation importance. By relegating otherworldly worth to creatures and nature, a few societies have added to the security of environments and the safeguarding of species.

Stewardship: Confidence in the holiness of creatures and the regular world frequently advances a feeling of stewardship and obligation regarding safeguarding the climate.

Biodiversity Preservation: Perceiving the significance of creatures in profound convictions can prompt a more prominent enthusiasm for biodiversity and endeavors to moderate species and their living spaces.

VIII. Contemporary Translations and Difficulties

In the advanced world, totemism and soul creatures keep on holding individual and social importance. In any case, these convictions are likewise met with difficulties and discussions.

Apportionment and Commercialization: The commercialization of tribal and otherworldly ideas, like selling "soul creature" stock, has raised worries about social appointment and the commodification of consecrated convictions.

Social Responsiveness: It is fundamental for people from non-native foundations to move toward totemism and soul creature ideas with social awareness and regard for the practices from which they are determined.

Natural Mindfulness: As biological worries develop, a few people focus on totemism and soul creatures as wellsprings of motivation for ecological activism and preservation endeavors.

2.1 Totemism: Ancestral Connections

Totemism is an intricate and multi-layered conviction framework that has been a vital piece of numerous native societies all over the planet. At its center, totemism includes the profound respect for and association with regular components, creatures, or plants, known as symbols. These symbols are accepted to typify the characteristics and traits of the related components and assume fundamental parts in the personality, culture, and otherworldliness of the networks that training totemism. This article dives into the complex snare of totemism, investigating its hereditary associations and the manners by which it shapes the convictions, customs, and perspective of native societies.

1. The Embodiment of Totemism

Characterizing Totemism

Totemism is a conviction framework that focuses on the reverence of emblems, which are viewed as hallowed and emblematically address creatures, plants, or other normal components. Symbols epitomize the characteristics, traits, and otherworldly meaning of the related components. The idea of totemism is in many cases established in the confidence in the interconnectedness of all living things and the otherworldly element of the regular world.

Familial Associations

Genealogical associations are at the core of totemism. These associations incorporate the accompanying components:

1. **Predecessors and Emblems:** Symbols are frequently connected with the precursors of a local area or clan. They act as profound gatekeepers and wellsprings of personality, helping people to remember their tribal roots.
2. **Connection and Genealogy:** Emblems are connected to connection frameworks, with explicit tribes or families embracing specific symbols. These emblems build up friendly securities and genealogical ties among local area individuals.

3. **Social Personality:** Emblems assume a critical part in molding the social character of native people groups, giving a feeling of having a place and shared legacy. The tribal images are frequently integrated into customs, workmanship, and narrating.

II. Totemism in Native Societies

Totemism has been rehearsed by various native societies around the world, each with its exceptional understandings and articulations of this conviction framework. While the particulars of totemism differ across societies, a few normal topics and practices can be recognized.

Local American Totemism

Local American societies are eminent for their rich custom of totemism. Emblems are much of the time creatures, like the bear, bird, or wolf, and they assume focal parts in otherworldliness, family relationship, and social association.

1. **Faction Symbols:** Numerous Local American clans are coordinated into tribes, with every group taking on a particular emblem creature. The individuals from a faction love their symbol as an indispensable piece of their more distant family.
2. **Command hierarchies:** Native clans of the Pacific Northwest, including the Haida and Tlingit, are known for their transcending command hierarchies. These figures, frequently cut from cedar, portray the emblems of a tribe or family and act as a visual portrayal of their tribal convictions and chronicles.

Native Australian Symbols

Totemism is likewise predominant in Native Australian societies. In these social orders, symbols are associated with the land and the Dreamtime, an otherworldly structure that makes sense of the production of the world and the beginnings of emblems.

1. **Family relationship and Symbols:** Emblems in Native societies are firmly connected to connection frameworks. Every individual has a place with at least one tribal gatherings, mirroring their character and jobs inside the local area.
2. **Dreamtime Stories:** Tribal convictions are interlaced with Dreamtime stories that hold significant otherworldly and social importance. These accounts are gone down through ages and are fundamental for safeguarding the way of life's set of experiences and values.

III. Totemism Past Native Societies

While totemism is generally regularly connected with native societies, the idea of emblems and hereditary associations stretches out past these networks.

Contemporary Totemism

In contemporary society, a few people and gatherings have taken on components of totemism as an approach to reconnect with nature, investigate otherworldliness, or embrace environmental qualities.

1. **Ecospirituality:** Ecospirituality is a cutting edge development that stresses the otherworldly association among people and the regular world, including creatures. It advances that all living things are interconnected and deserving of regard.
2. **New Age Totemism:** Certain individuals inside the New Age development look to interface with creature symbols as wellsprings of direction, recuperating, and self-improvement. These emblems might be related with explicit individual characteristics or qualities.

Totemism in Mainstream society

The imagery of totemism has advanced into mainstream society, where creature emblems are frequently utilized as images and themes.

1. **Sports Groups:** Many games groups embrace creature mascots and emblems, integrating these images into their marking and personalities. These mascots frequently address characteristics like strength, spryness, or cooperation.
2. **Imagery in Writing and Film:** In writing and film, creatures are often utilized as images to convey more profound implications or subjects. For instance, the lion in "The Lion Lord" is an image of boldness and initiative.

IV. Genealogical Associations and Social Character

Totemism significantly shapes the social personality of native networks by laying out an association among people and their precursors.

Genealogical Watchmen

Emblems are viewed as hereditary watchmen, exemplifying the insight and force of the individuals who preceded. This association with the past is an indication of the getting through presence of progenitors inside the local area.

Family relationship and Heredity

Emblems are personally connected to family relationship frameworks and heredity. Family emblems are passed down starting with one age then onto the next, supporting the genealogical ties among local area individuals. The family relationship in view of tribal affiliations frames the premise of social association and collaboration.

Individual Personality

Tribal affiliations shape individual personalities inside the local area. A singular's emblem is a piece of their character, a wellspring of pride, and an association with the predecessors. These affiliations are in many cases celebrated and supported through customs, narrating, and services.

V. Customs and Services

Totemism is intently attached to customs and services that celebrate tribal associations and insist the otherworldly meaning of emblems.

Naming Services

In certain societies, an individual's symbol creature might impact their name, highlighting the profound association and meaning of the emblem in a singular's life.

Soul changing experiences

Tribal topics are woven into soul changing experiences, like transitioning services and commencements. These customs mark critical life advances and effectively associate people with their tribal roots.

Mending and Insurance

Emblems are frequently conjured for mending services and insurance ceremonies. Shamans and medication individuals might call upon the force of emblem creatures to help with their work, looking for direction and profound help.

VI. Social Protection

Totemism assumes an essential part in protecting the social legacy and upsides of native networks.

Narrating and Oral Customs

The convictions and customs related with emblems are gone down through ages by means of narrating and oral practices. These stories help to save the social history and upsides of the local area.

Workmanship and Articulation

Symbols are in many cases portrayed in different types of workmanship, including carvings, compositions, and materials. This creative articulation effectively builds up the profound and social meaning of symbols and familial associations.

VII. Difficulties and Contemporary Discussions

Totemism faces a scope of difficulties and contemporary discussions in the cutting edge world.

Social Assignment

The commercialization of tribal and profound ideas, like selling "soul creature" stock, has raised worries about social apportionment and the commodification of consecrated convictions.

Social Responsiveness

It is fundamental for people from non-native foundations to move toward totemism with social responsiveness and regard for the practices from which it is inferred. Tribal convictions are well established in the way of life and otherworldliness of native networks, and pariahs ought to draw in with these convictions with mindfulness and lowliness.

Biological Mindfulness

As biological worries develop, a few people focus on totemism as a wellspring of motivation for natural activism and protection endeavors. Perceiving the interconnectedness of all living things and the otherworldly meaning of emblems can encourage a more noteworthy enthusiasm for biodiversity and endeavors to save species and their environments.

2.2Guardian Spirits and Familiars

All through mankind's set of experiences, the faith in watchman spirits and familiars has been an ongoing idea in different societies and conviction frameworks. These mysterious connections among people and creatures uncover the profound association that exists between our species and the set of all animals. Gatekeeper spirits and familiars act as defenders, guides, and wellsprings of profound knowledge. This article dives into the significant connections among people and these creature partners, investigating their importance in various social settings and conviction frameworks.

1. **Gatekeeper Spirits: Profound Defenders**

Gatekeeper spirits, otherwise called soul creatures or creature guides, are accepted to be defensive spirits that watch over and guide people. These spirits are frequently connected with creatures and are viewed as wellsprings of solidarity, insight, and direction.

Native Conviction Frameworks

Watchman spirits assume a critical part in different native conviction frameworks. In numerous native societies, it is accepted that people have at least one gatekeeper spirits that secure and direct them all through their lives.

1. **Local American Gatekeeper Spirits:** Local American clans have long held the faith in watchman spirits, which are frequently connected with explicit creatures. These spirits act as defenders and wellsprings of individual power, and people might set out on vision missions to interface with their gatekeeper spirits.
2. **African Gatekeeper Spirits:** In numerous African societies, people accept that they have individual watchman spirits as creatures. These spirits are accepted to offer security and direction and are many times uncovered through dreams, dreams, or initiatory encounters.

Shamanic Practices

Shamanic customs frequently include the conjuring of watchman spirits to work with recuperating, divination, and profound excursions.

1. **Creature Soul Guides:** Shamans in different societies work with creature soul advisers for associate with the soul world, look for understanding, and saddle

the power and characteristics of the creatures they work with. These creature guides are viewed as go-betweens between the human and soul domains.

2. **Power Creatures:** Power creatures, a subset of watchman spirits, are explicit creatures that are especially connected with a person. These creatures are accepted to grant explicit characteristics, qualities, and bits of knowledge to the individual.

II. Familiars: Mystical Associates

Familiars are mysterious creature mates that have been a piece of Western elusive and mystical practices for a really long time. These creatures are accepted to help specialists in their supernatural undertakings and act as mediators between the physical and profound domains.

Authentic Beginnings

The idea of familiars can be followed back to the black magic preliminaries of the Early Current time frame, when witches were blamed for having creature familiars that supported them in their alleged dim practices. Familiars were frequently accepted to be spirits or extraordinary substances that took on creature structures.

Contemporary Practice

In current black magic and neopagan customs, familiars are many times seen as lively or otherworldly partners that help professionals in their mysterious work. These familiars might appear as actual creatures or exist absolutely in the profound domain.

1. **Bond with Actual Creatures:** A few professionals lay out a profound otherworldly bond with their actual pets, thinking of them as familiars. These creatures are accepted to have an increased mindfulness and association with the profound world.
2. **Mystical Work:** Familiars are frequently called after during ceremonies, divination, and spellwork to help the expert. They might be accepted to offer assurance, understanding, and direction in supernatural undertakings.

III. Social Importance

Gatekeeper spirits and familiars hold social importance in various ways, mirroring the qualities, convictions, and practices of the social orders and conviction frameworks that revere them.

Local American Culture

In Local American societies, watchman spirits are a wellspring of otherworldly strength, shrewdness, and individual power. They are firmly connected to the regular world and the interconnectedness of all living things.

1. **Connection and Symbols:** Gatekeeper spirits are frequently connected with explicit creature emblems, which are shared by individuals from a family or

clan. These emblems build up the feeling of family relationship and association among local area individuals.

2. **Custom and Function:** Local American ceremonies and services frequently include the conjuring of gatekeeper spirits, as well as moves and ceremonies that praise the otherworldly association among people and creatures.

African Conviction Frameworks

In African societies, gatekeeper spirits are personally associated with the profound domain and are accepted to offer security, direction, and knowledge.

1. **Individual Soul Creatures:** People frequently have their very own gatekeeper spirits, accepted to be creature spirits that watch over and guide them. These spirits are uncovered through dreams, dreams, and initiatory encounters.
2. **Genealogical Associations:** Gatekeeper spirits in African societies are firmly connected with familial associations and are viewed as middle people between the living and the soul world.

Western Recondite Practices

Familiars in Western recondite and supernatural customs have been related with black magic, the mysterious, and enchanted rehearses for quite a long time.

1. **Witch Preliminaries:** During the witch preliminaries of the Early Present day time frame, familiars were in many cases key to allegations of black magic. These creatures were accepted to be friends of witches and members in their alleged dim ceremonies.
2. **Present day Black magic:** In contemporary black magic and neopagan customs, familiars act as supernatural friends and partners, helping experts in their spellwork, divination, and ceremonies.

IV. The Connection Among People and Their Creature Partners

The connection among people and their watchman spirits or familiars is described by profound and complex connections that are molded by trust, respect, and correspondence.

Trust and Correspondence

In native societies, the relationship with gatekeeper spirits is based on trust and correspondence. People look for direction and security from their spirits and speak with them through customs, functions, and dreams.

Correspondence

There is in many cases a feeling of correspondence in the connection among people and gatekeeper spirits or familiars. People honor and care for their creature partners, and consequently, they get assurance, direction, and backing in different parts of life.

Profound Association

The connection among people and their creature partners is established in a significant profound association. This association goes past the actual domain and reaches out into the profound or enthusiastic aspects, considering a scaffold between the human and soul universes.

V. The Job of Creatures in Present day culture

In contemporary society, the meaning of watchman spirits and familiars stretches out past native societies and mystical practices.

Natural Mindfulness

As natural worries develop, a few people focus on their gatekeeper spirits or familiars as wellsprings of motivation for ecological activism and protection endeavors. The confidence in the interconnectedness of all living things and the otherworldly meaning of creatures can encourage a more prominent enthusiasm for biodiversity and endeavors to monitor species and their environments.

Self-improvement and Strengthening

The confidence in gatekeeper spirits and familiars is frequently connected with self-awareness and strengthening. Numerous people track down strength, knowledge, and direction in their profound associations with creatures, which can enable them to explore life's difficulties and vulnerabilities.

Moral Contemplations

The act of creature wizardry and the summon of watchman spirits and familiars raise moral contemplations. People genuinely should move toward these practices with deference for the creatures in question and to guarantee their prosperity and government assistance.

2.3 Animal Spirits in Shamanism

Shamanism, one of the world's most established otherworldly practices, is portrayed by its profound association with nature and the confidence in creature spirits as middle people between the human and soul universes. In shamanic customs, creatures are viewed as something other than animals; they are loved as strong and savvy creatures with the capacity to direct, recuperate, and secure. This exposition investigates the rich embroidered artwork of creature spirits in shamanism, analyzing their job, imagery, and importance in different societies and conviction frameworks.

1. **Grasping Shamanism**
   Meaning of Shamanism
   Shamanism is a profound and mending practice that goes back millennia and is tracked down in societies all over the planet. It is described by the faith in the capacity of shamans, profound experts, to associate with the soul world to work

with recuperating, divination, and direction. Creatures assume an essential part in shamanic rehearses as they are accepted to be the extension between the physical and profound domains.

The Job of the Shaman

Shamans are otherworldly pioneers and healers who enter adjusted conditions of cognizance to speak with the soul world. They are many times thought about go-betweens among people and the soul domain, and they utilize their association with soul creatures to work with recuperating, divination, and other profound practices.

2. **Creature Spirits in Shamanic Conviction Frameworks**

Creature spirits are a foundation of shamanic conviction frameworks across societies. These spirits are accepted to have characteristics and astuteness that can help shamans and their networks in different ways.

Local American Shamanism

Local American shamanism, with its rich practice of creature spirits, is a notable illustration of the confidence in creature partners. In these societies, creatures are viewed as guides, defenders, and wellsprings of force.

1. **Symbol Creatures:** Local American clans frequently have emblem creatures related with factions or families. These emblem creatures are loved as familial spirits and are accepted to offer direction and insurance to their human partners.
2. **Vision Journeys:** Vision missions are a focal piece of Local American shamanism. During these missions, people look for contact with their soul creatures and get direction and understanding for their lives.

Siberian Shamanism

Siberian shamanism is one more old custom that puts major areas of strength for an on the meaning of creature spirits. In Siberian societies, the shaman's association with creatures is accepted to be a wellspring of force and mending.

1. **Soul Guides:** Siberian shamans frequently have creature soul directs that help them in their otherworldly work. These aides are accepted to assist shamans with exploring the soul world, mend the wiped out, and perform divination.
2. **Bear Service:** The bear holds an extraordinary spot in Siberian shamanism, and the Bear Function is a custom that looks to guarantee the prosperity of the local area. The bear is viewed as a defender and wellspring of solidarity.

African Shamanism

African shamanic customs additionally integrate creature spirits into their conviction frameworks. In these societies, creatures are viewed as the two aides and defenders, offering their insight and capacity to the people who look for it.

1. **Individual Soul Creatures:** Numerous African societies accept that people have individual soul creatures. These creatures act as defenders, offering direction and backing in different parts of life.
2. **Hereditary Spirits:** Creatures are frequently connected with tribal spirits in African shamanism. They are accepted to be mediators between the living and the soul world, interfacing individuals with their progenitors.

III. Imagery of Creature Spirits in Shamanism

The imagery of creature spirits in shamanism shifts across societies, yet normal subjects and qualities can be distinguished.

Strength and Power

Numerous creature spirits in shamanism are related with strength and power. These creatures are viewed as wellsprings of physical and profound strength, frequently furnishing shamans with the energy and mettle required for their mending and divination work.

Intelligence and Direction

Creature spirits are loved for their insight and the direction they deal to shamans and their networks. These spirits are accepted to have profound understanding into the regular world and the soul domain, and they give significant direction in different parts of life.

Security and Mending

Creature spirits are frequently conjured for security and mending in shamanic ceremonies. They are accepted to safeguard people and networks from hurt and to help with the course of physical and profound recuperating.

Change

The possibility of change is a common topic in shamanism, and creatures that go through critical changes in their day to day existence cycles are frequently worshipped as images of progress and recharging. The butterfly, for instance, is viewed as an image of individual change and development.

IV. Shamanic Practices and Ceremonies

Shamanic practices and ceremonies are profoundly interlaced with the presence of creature spirits. These practices associate the shaman and their local area with the soul world and to tackle the power and intelligence of creature partners.

Creature Emblems

In numerous shamanic customs, creature emblems assume a huge part. Emblem creatures are viewed as hereditary spirits and act as guides and defenders. They are in many cases summoned in customs, moves, and functions to look for their insight and endowments.

Vision Missions

Vision missions are a focal practice in shamanism, particularly in Local American and Siberian customs. During a dream mission, people look for contact with their soul creatures and get bits of knowledge and direction. These missions are frequently joined by fasting, contemplation, and time spent in nature.

Mending Ceremonies

Shamans often call upon creature spirits to help with mending ceremonies. These ceremonies might include the utilization of explicit creature symbolism or the summon of creature spirits to help analyze and treat disease. Creature spirits are accepted to furnish the shaman with the information and power required for compelling recuperating.

Divination

Divination is a typical shamanic practice that includes looking for experiences from the soul world. Creature spirits are frequently counseled to give answers and direction in divination practices like perusing creature bones, shells, or other regular items.

V. Biological and Otherworldly Importance

The faith in creature spirits in shamanism conveys both natural and otherworldly importance.

Biological Mindfulness

Shamanic customs frequently stress the interconnectedness of all living things, including creatures. This biological mindfulness supports a profound regard for nature and every one of its occupants and cultivates a feeling of stewardship for the climate.

Profound Association

Shamanism underscores the otherworldly association among people and creatures, mirroring a confidence in the reliance of every single living being. This association fills in as a sign of the holiness of the normal world and the significance of keeping up with concordance with it.

VI. Difficulties and Contemporary Transformations

In the cutting edge world, the act of shamanism and the faith in creature spirits face different difficulties and transformations.

Social Appointment

The commercialization of shamanic rehearses and the appointment of native practices have raised worries about social awareness and regard. It is fundamental for people to draw in with shamanism with deference for the social and profound legacy of the networks from which it starts.

Protection and Morals

As natural worries develop, a few people shift focus over to shamanism as a wellspring of motivation for ecological activism and protection endeavors. This association between shamanic convictions and protection highlights the significance of moral contemplations and regard for the regular world.

Present day Variations

Shamanic rehearses have tracked down their place in contemporary otherworldly developments and self-improvement. While customary shamanism stays a significant and regarded practice, current variations consolidate shamanic components into self-awareness and recuperating rehearses.

Chapter 3

The Cosmic Menagerie: Animals in Creation Myths

Creation fantasies are old stories that try to make sense of the starting points of the world, the universe, and mankind. They are fundamental parts of different societies, filling in as a method for conveying the convictions, values, and perspectives of various social orders. A common and spellbinding topic in these fantasies is the job of creatures. Creatures are in many cases depicted as focal characters, holy creatures, or guardian angels in creation stories. This exposition investigates the grandiose zoo of creatures in creation fantasies, featuring their importance in forming social stories, profound convictions, and our comprehension of the world's starting points.

1. **The Comprehensiveness of Creation Legends**
   Creation fantasies are tracked down in societies all over the planet, making them a general and getting through part of human narrating. In spite of their social variety, these fantasies frequently share normal topics, remembering the contribution of creatures for the demonstration of creation.
   Shared Subjects
   Numerous creation fantasies, independent of their social starting points, share normal components, like the production of the world, the development of mankind, and the intercession of powerful creatures or divine beings. Creatures regularly assume key parts in these accounts.
   Varieties in Legendary Topics
   Despite the fact that there are shared topics, creation legends vary generally in their particular subtleties, characters, and imagery. This variety mirrors the remarkable social and topographical settings in which these fantasies have created.
2. **Creatures as Makers and Shapers of Universes**

Creatures in creation legends frequently act as dynamic members in the creation and forming of the world. Their activities, qualities, and imagery add to the account of how the universe appeared.

Old Egyptian Creation Fantasy

In the old Egyptian creation fantasy, the universe was brought into the world from the tumultuous waters of the antiquated sea, Sister. The god Atum, addressed as a snake, rose up out of this watery void. Atum's demonstration of self-creation represents the groundbreaking force of the snake, a theme tracked down in many societies.

1. **Imagery of the Snake:** The snake in this creation legend addresses recovery, change, and recurrent resurrection. It is an indication of the steadily developing nature of the universe.

Hindu Creation Legend

In Hinduism, the Rigveda, quite possibly of the most seasoned sacrosanct text, contains creation legends that include the grandiose penance of the god Purusha. This penance prompts the making of different components of the world, including creatures, which are a fundamental piece of the conciliatory custom.

1. **Creature Penance:** The penance of creatures in this creation fantasy is emblematic of the interconnectedness of all living things. The creatures presented in the custom address various parts of the world, from the sky to the earth.

Maori Creation Fantasy

The Maori nation of New Zealand have a creation fantasy that recounts the sky father Ranginui and the earth mother Papatuanuku, who were isolated by their youngsters, making the space for the world as far as we might be concerned. In this legend, creatures are relatives of the kids who made the world.

1. **Creatures as Family members:** In the Maori fantasy, creatures are viewed as family members, relatives of the divine beings. This point of view stresses the interconnectedness of people, creatures, and the earth.

III. Creatures as Hallowed Images

Creatures in creation legends are frequently enriched with emblematic importance that rises above their actual attributes. These images might address temperances, characteristics, or enormous powers.

Chinese Creation Fantasy

In Chinese folklore, the formation of the world is ascribed to the grandiose egg, from which Pangu, the main human, arose. Pangu's demonstration of creation is much of the time addressed close by other vast creatures, like the phoenix and the mythical beast.

1. **Imagery of the Phoenix:** The phoenix is an image of resurrection and everlasting status. Its presence in the creation fantasy highlights the repeating idea of creation and the restoration of life.
2. **Imagery of the Mythical beast:** The winged serpent addresses astronomical powers and early stage power. It is related with the harmony between Yin and Yang and the molding of the universe.

Local American Creation Fantasies

Local American creation fantasies are different, mirroring the rich embroidery of native societies across the Americas. In a large number of these legends, creatures hold a consecrated spot on the planet's creation.

1. **The Navajo and the Coyote:** In Navajo creation stories, the Coyote is a focal person and a comedian figure. The Coyote's activities and experiences shape the world and its scenes, exemplifying the lively and innovative soul of the universe.
2. **The Haida and the Raven:** Among the Haida nation of the Pacific Northwest, the Raven is a vital figure in creation stories. The Raven is both a maker and a transformer, forming the world and carrying light to the murkiness.

IV. Creature Imagery in Human Beginnings

Numerous creation legends include creatures as vital to the beginnings of humankind. In these stories, creatures frequently hold an extraordinary job in the making of people.

African Creation Fantasies

In African creation fantasies, creatures assume a critical part in the making of people. A few legends recount how creatures and people were once something similar, and it was through a course of change that people became particular from creatures.

1. **San Bushmen and the Mantis:** The San Bushmen of southern Africa have a creation fantasy including the Mantis, a heavenly figure who formed the main people. The Mantis is both a maker and a prankster, mirroring the intricacy of human instinct.
2. **Yoruba and the Ori:** In Yoruba folklore, the god Ori is related with individual predetermination and the head. Ori is represented by the bird, and it is accepted that people accept their predeterminations from the Ori.

Local American Creation Legends

A few Local American creation legends likewise consolidate creatures in the beginning of humankind. These legends stress the interconnectedness of people and creatures.

1. **The Ojibwa and the Turtle:** In Ojibwa creation stories, the world is frequently depicted as laying on the rear of a turtle. The turtle represents the primary job of creatures in supporting the world.
2. **The Hopi and the Subterranean insect Individuals:** The Hopi public have a creation legend that recounts the Subterranean insect Individuals, who aided cover the Hopi from calamitous occasions. The Insect Public are representative of lowliness and the significance of cooperating with other living things.

V. Creatures as Couriers and Guides

Creatures in creation legends frequently act as couriers or guides who help people in their connections with the heavenly or powerful domains. These creatures go about as middle people between the human and soul universes.

Norse Creation Legend

In Norse folklore, the astronomical tree Yggdrasil is occupied by different animals, including the falcon at the most elevated branch, the snake at the roots, and the squirrel that hastens all over the tree. These creatures assume parts as couriers and guides.

1. **The Hawk:** The falcon addresses the association between the sky and the earth. It fills in as a courier between the divine beings in the heavenly domain and the natural domain.
2. **The Snake:** The snake represents the hidden world and the pattern of death and resurrection. It is related with astuteness and information.
3. **The Squirrel:** The squirrel goes about as a courier, conveying news and tattle between the falcon at the highest point of the tree and the snake at the roots.

Australian Native Creation Legends

Australian Native creation legends frequently highlight creatures as hereditary creatures and guides. These creatures significantly affect the scene and on the existences of people.

1. **The Rainbow Snake:** The Rainbow Snake is a typical figure in Australian Native creation legends. It is related with the formation of streams, landforms, and the restoration of life. The Rainbow Snake is viewed as an aide and defender of the land.
2. **Tribal Creatures:** In Native societies, tribal creatures are accepted to be the progenitors of people and act as guides and defenders. These creatures are integrated into the social and profound character of people and networks.

VI. Moral Examples and Moral Qualities

Creation fantasies frequently pass moral examples and moral qualities on through the activities and ways of behaving of creatures. These fantasies give social structures to grasping the jobs and obligations of people on the planet.

Aesop's Tales

Aesop's Tales, an assortment of old Greek stories, use creatures as characters to convey moral illustrations and moral qualities. These tales have risen above their starting points and remain commonly known and esteemed for their persevering through astuteness.

1. **The Turtle and the Bunny:** This tale shows the worth of steadiness and lowliness. The sluggish turtle comes out on top in the race against the presumptuous rabbit, representing the significance of persistence and consistency.
2. **The Kid Who Told a shameful lie:** In this tale, a young man dishonestly guarantees that a wolf is going after the town. At the point when a genuine wolf at last shows up, nobody trusts him. The story conveys the outcomes of unscrupulousness and the significance of believability.

Native Moral Examples

Native societies frequently integrate creatures into their creation fantasies to convey moral examples and moral qualities.

1. **The Pueblo and the Hummingbird:** In Pueblo culture, the hummingbird is an image of affection and empathy. The narrative of the hummingbird shows the benefit of really focusing on others and cooperating to make the world a superior spot.
2. **The Lakota and the White Bison Calf Lady:** The White Bison Calf Lady is a hallowed figure in Lakota folklore who carries significant lessons to individuals. Her story accentuates values like regard for nature, local area, and otherworldliness.

VII. Ecological Mindfulness

Creation legends, with their veneration for creatures and the regular world, frequently advance natural mindfulness and a feeling of stewardship for the Earth.

African Creation Fantasies

African creation fantasies every now and again feature the significance of living as one with the normal world. These legends frequently underline the interconnectedness of people, creatures, and the climate.

1. **San Bushmen and the Eland:** In San Bushmen folklore, the eland is a consecrated creature. The eland's part in creation is a sign of the holiness of nature and the need to safeguard and regard the climate.
2. **Yoruba and the Rainforest:** The Yoruba public have a creation fantasy in which the rainforest is related with the heavenly. This fantasy highlights the significance of safeguarding the rainforest and its biodiversity.

Local American Creation Legends

Local American creation legends likewise underscore the interconnectedness of people and the regular world, advancing a feeling of ecological stewardship.

1. **The Haida and the Raven:** The Haida public accept that the Raven carried light to the world. The story underlines the significance of light and the equilibrium of nature.
2. **The Hopi and the Insect Public:** The Hopi creation fantasy including the Subterranean insect Individuals conveys the significance of lowliness and cooperating with other living things. It fills in as a sign of the need to regard and really focus on the Earth.

VIII. Difficulties and Contemporary Transformations

While creation fantasies give social and profound direction, they likewise face difficulties and variations in the cutting edge world.

Social Apportionment

The apportionment of native creation fantasies and the commercialization of their images have raised worries about social awareness and regard for the customs from which these accounts start. It is vital for people to draw in with these legends with deference for the social and otherworldly legacy of native networks.

Preservation Endeavors

The association between creation fantasies and ecological mindfulness highlights the significance of protection endeavors. Numerous native networks are effectively engaged with preservation drives, trying to safeguard the normal world and its biodiversity.

Current Transformations

In contemporary society, the subjects of creation fantasies keep on affecting craftsmanship, writing, and mainstream society. These variations mirror a craving to interface with the insight and imagery tracked down in these old stories.

3.1 World-Forming Beasts

All through mankind's set of experiences, fantasies and legends have highlighted a wide exhibit of legendary animals that assumed vital parts in forming the world and the universe. These world-framing monsters are frequently invested with uncommon powers, epitomizing the imaginative and disastrous powers that oversee the universe.

They show up in the creation fantasies and accounts of assorted societies, each adding to the social and otherworldly comprehension of the universe. This exposition dives into the universe of world-framing monsters, investigating their importance and imagery in various customs, and what they have meant for human points of view on the universe and the powers that oversee it.

1. **The Force of Legendary Animals**
   Legendary animals, frequently portrayed as creatures with godlike characteristics, have long interested human creative mind. They act as both model images and characters in stories that convey social qualities and convictions.
   Imagery of Legendary Animals
   Legendary animals frequently represent basic parts of presence, like creation, annihilation, change, and the equilibrium of powers known to mankind. Their imagery shifts across societies, mirroring the novel viewpoints of various social orders.
   Prototype Importance
   Legendary animals address prototype figures that repeat in the aggregate unaware of humankind. These originals epitomize general subjects and encounters, making them appealing and ageless with regards to human culture.
2. **The Job of World-Framing Monsters**

World-framing monsters are legendary animals that hold the ability to shape the universe and the world. They are in many cases focal characters in creation legends, where their activities and qualities impact the creation and request of the universe.

The Enormous Egg and the Phoenix

In different societies, the idea of the enormous egg is key to creation legends. It addresses the basic reality from which the universe arises. The inestimable egg is frequently connected with the phoenix, a world-framing monster known for its capacity to recharge and reproduce the world through its searing resurrection.

1. **Hindu Creation Fantasy:** In Hinduism, the grandiose egg addresses the early stage condition of the universe. The god Vishnu rises up out of this egg and proceeds to make and shape the world.
2. **Egyptian Creation Fantasy:** The phoenix is related with the sun god Ra in Egyptian folklore. It is accepted that the phoenix is reawakened from the cinders of its ancestor, representing the timeless pattern of death and resurrection, which is a basic part of creation.

The World Turtle

The world turtle is a typical theme in creation legends, especially in South Asian and Local American societies. In these legends, the world lays on the rear of a monstrous turtle, underscoring the interconnectedness of the Earth with the universe.

1. **Hindu Creation Legend:** In Hinduism, the world turtle is accepted to help the Earth, representing the primary job of creatures and legendary animals in the construction of the universe.
2. **Local American Creation Fantasy:** The idea of the world turtle is available in different Local American creation legends. It is related with equilibrium and concordance between the normal and otherworldly universes.

The Snake and the Mythical beast

Snakes and winged serpents are unmistakable world-shaping monsters in numerous social legends. They frequently represent the double idea of creation and obliteration, as well as the recurrent powers that oversee the universe.

1. **Norse Creation Legend:** The Midgard Snake, an enormous snake, circles the world in Norse folklore. Its presence represents the double idea of creation and obliteration, as it both maintains and compromises the world.
2. **Chinese Creation Fantasy:** In Chinese folklore, the winged serpent is an image of grandiose powers and early stage power. It assumes a pivotal part in the creation and request of the universe.

III. Imagery and Importance

World-framing monsters in creation fantasies hold rich imagery and profound social importance, adding to the comprehension of the universe and the powers that shape it.

Creation and Annihilation

The presence of world-framing monsters frequently means the duality of creation and annihilation. These animals, whether snakes, mythical beasts, or phoenixes, encapsulate the powers that achieve both the birth and the finish of universes.

Equilibrium and Agreement

World-framing monsters underscore the requirement for equilibrium and congruity in the universe. The world turtle, for instance, means the significance of interconnectedness and the possibility that all living things are indispensable to the grandiose request.

Repeating Nature of the Universe

Numerous world-shaping monsters, like the phoenix and the snake, encapsulate the recurrent idea of the universe. They address the timeless pattern of death and resurrection, representing the ceaseless restoration and change of the universe.

IV. Social Viewpoints on World-Shaping Monsters

Various societies offer extraordinary viewpoints on world-framing monsters, mirroring their own qualities, convictions, and cosmologies. These viewpoints shed light on the variety of human idea and comprehension of the universe.

Chinese Viewpoint

In Chinese folklore, mythical beasts assume a focal part in creation and the vast request. They represent enormous powers and address the harmony between Yin and Yang, fundamental standards in Chinese cosmology.

1. **Yin and Yang:** Winged serpents are many times portrayed two by two, representing the amicable exchange of Yin and Yang, the dualistic powers that keep up with balance in the universe.
2. **Watchmen of Vast Equilibrium:** Mythical serpents are viewed as gatekeepers of inestimable equilibrium, guaranteeing the balance of the regular and profound universes.

Norse Point of view

In Norse folklore, the Midgard Snake circles the world, filling in as both a danger and a defender. It represents the possibility that creation and annihilation are entwined in the enormous request.

1. **Ragnarök:** The Midgard Snake's job in Norse folklore is especially clear during Ragnarök, the prophetically catastrophic occasion in which it fights with the god Thor, at last prompting the apocalypse.
2. **Pattern of Creation and Obliteration:** The presence of the snake builds up the Norse faith in the recurrent idea of the universe, where the finish of one world prompts the formation of another.

Hindu Point of view

In Hinduism, the enormous egg and the god Vishnu's arising out of it are fundamental to the creation fantasy. The infinite egg addresses the basic condition of the universe and the potential for its continuous creation.

1. **Resurrection and Recharging:** The idea of the enormous egg and Vishnu's development typify the thoughts of rebirth and reestablishment, underscoring the cyclic idea of the universe.
2. **Numerous Universes:** Hindu cosmology imagines the presence of various universes, each rising up out of the grandiose egg and at last getting back to it in a ceaseless pattern of creation and obliteration.

V. Moral and Philosophical Ramifications

World-shaping monsters in creation fantasies have moral and philosophical ramifications, offering bits of knowledge into the human mission for significance and comprehension of the universe.

Moral Illustrations

The presence of world-shaping monsters frequently conveys moral illustrations, underscoring the significance of equilibrium, congruity, and regard for the normal world. These examples resound with social qualities that advance mindful stewardship of the Earth.

Philosophical Reflections

World-shaping monsters welcome philosophical consideration about the idea of presence, the pattern of life and passing, and the interconnectedness of every single living being. They challenge people to consider their position in the universe and their part in keeping up with its harmony.

VI. Difficulties and Contemporary Understandings

The meaning of world-framing monsters in creation fantasies faces difficulties and variations in the cutting edge world. As societies advance and otherworldly points of view change, the pertinence of these fantasies keeps on being reconsidered and rethought.

Social Allotment

The allotment of world-shaping monsters and their imagery in business and well known settings has raised worries about social awareness and regard for the practices from which these legends begin. It is fundamental for people to move toward these fantasies with a comprehension of their social and profound legacy.

Ecological Mindfulness

The association between world-shaping monsters and natural mindfulness highlights the significance of preservation endeavors. Many societies that love these animals are effectively engaged with safeguarding the normal world and its biodiversity.

Contemporary Transformations

World-framing monsters keep on motivating contemporary craftsmanship, writing, and narrating. Their imagery stays important with regards to current translations, adding to progressing conversations about the powers that shape the universe and our job inside it.

3.2 Animal Deities and their Roles in Creation

Across societies and since forever ago, creatures play had a significant impact in the folklore and otherworldliness of human social orders. They have been adored, represented, and idolized as heavenly creatures with the ability to make and shape the world. These creature gods are focal characters in creation accounts, addressing the powers and properties that brought forth the universe. This paper investigates the jobs and meaning of creature divinities in creation fantasies from various regions of the planet, revealing insight into the different manners by which these creatures have formed the social and otherworldly comprehension of the starting points of the universe.

1. **The Comprehensiveness of Creature Gods**
   The worship of creatures as gods is a boundless peculiarity tracked down in various societies across the globe. While explicit creatures and their jobs might fluctuate, the idea of creatures as heavenly creatures with imaginative power is a widespread topic in human folklore.
   Normal Components
   Creation fantasies highlighting creature divinities frequently share normal components, including the attribution of phenomenal characteristics, the job of these creatures in forming the universe, and their encapsulation of astronomical powers.
   Different Social Articulations
   While there are shared topics, the variety of social articulations in creation fantasies is huge, reflecting extraordinary points of view, values, and convictions inside every general public.
2. **Creature Gods and Their Jobs in Creation**

Creature gods hold different jobs in the creation stories of various societies. They address a large number of properties and inestimable powers, adding to the development and request of the universe.

The Egyptian Pantheon and the Consecrated Scarab

In old Egypt, the consecrated scarab bug, known as Khepri or "the person who appears," is an unmistakable creature divinity with an imperative job in creation.

1. **Job in Creation:** Khepri is related with the rising sun and the making of the world. It is accepted that Khepri pushes the sun across the sky every day, representing the restoration of life and the resurrection of the universe.
2. **Imagery:** The scarab bug, with its propensity for moving wads of excrement, addresses the recurrent idea of creation and the idea of recovery. The scarab's capacity to change rotting matter into life mirrors the possibility of change and reestablishment.

The Hindu Pantheon and the Heavenly Cow

In Hinduism, the heavenly cow Kamadhenu, frequently alluded to as "the wish-satisfying cow," holds a huge job in creation and food.

1. **Job in Creation:** Kamadhenu is accepted to have arisen during the beating of the grandiose sea, a urgent occasion in Hindu folklore. She is the wellspring of all natural riches and sustenance, exemplifying the overflow that supports the universe.

2. **Imagery:** Kamadhenu addresses ripeness, sustenance, and the sustaining parts of creation. She is venerated as the mother of all cows and is related with the ability to give wishes and satisfy wants.

The Chinese Practice and the Heavenly Mythical serpent

In Chinese folklore, the winged serpent is a venerated creature divinity with a focal job in creation stories.

1. **Job in Creation:** Winged serpents are viewed as heavenly creatures related with water and the production of streams, lakes, and the seas. The winged serpent's job in controlling water is crucial to the arrangement and request of the world.
2. **Imagery:** The mythical serpent represents inestimable powers, basic power, and the harmony among paradise and earth. It addresses the repetitive idea of creation and is an image of royal power and the ruler's heavenly association.

The Norse Custom and the World-Snake

In Norse folklore, the world-snake Jörmungandr is a fundamental creature god with a critical job in the creation and request of the universe.

1. **Job in Creation:** Jörmungandr is accepted to circle the world, maintaining a level of control and keeping it from going to pieces. Its presence in Norse cosmology is fundamental to keeping up with the equilibrium and design of the universe.
2. **Imagery:** The world-snake represents the double idea of creation and annihilation. While it adds to the enormous request by forestalling tumult, it likewise addresses the disastrous powers that will assume a part in the calamitous occasions of Ragnarök.

III. Imagery and Importance

The imagery and meaning of creature divinities in creation legends are different and multi-layered. They epitomize different properties and infinite powers that add to the development and request of the universe.

Creation and Food

Creature gods frequently represent the imaginative and sustaining parts of the universe. They are related with the introduction of the world, the recharging of life, and the overflow that supports generally living creatures.

Astronomical Powers

Creature divinities address infinite powers that oversee the universe. These powers incorporate the sun, water, fruitfulness, and the patterns of creation and obliteration.

Double Nature

Numerous creature divinities exemplify a double nature, addressing both creation and obliteration. This duality highlights that the powers forming the universe are multi-layered and interwoven.

IV. Social Points of view on Creature Divinities

Various societies offer exceptional points of view on creature gods, mirroring their own qualities, convictions, and cosmologies. These points of view give knowledge into the variety of human idea and comprehension of the beginnings of the universe.

Hindu Point of view

In Hinduism, the idea of the heavenly cow, Kamadhenu, represents overflow, sustenance, and the job of the maternal in creation. Kamadhenu's importance stretches out to the possibility of dharma (obligation) and the interconnectedness of all living things.

1. **Overflow and Sustenance:** Kamadhenu encapsulates the possibility of overflow, giving sustenance and abundance to every single living being. This imagery features the significance of food in the vast request.
2. **Dharma and Interconnectedness:** Kamadhenu's job as the mother of all cows stresses the interconnectedness of living things and the idea of dharma, where each being has an obligation in the excellent plan of creation.

Chinese Viewpoint

In Chinese folklore, winged serpents are viewed as divine creatures with the ability to control water and keep the vast control. They represent the harmony among paradise and earth and address the sovereign's heavenly power.

1. **Water and Vast Equilibrium:** Winged serpents are related with water, representing its life-supporting properties. The control of water is fundamental to keeping up with the equilibrium and request of the universe.
2. **Supreme Power:** Winged serpents are emblematic of majestic power and the head's heavenly association. Their presence in Chinese culture highlights the possibility of an agreeable and very much arranged world.

Norse Viewpoint

In Norse folklore, the world-snake Jörmungandr exemplifies the double idea of creation and obliteration, as it the two keeps the world intact and assumes a part in its possible obliteration during Ragnarök.

1. **Grandiose Equilibrium and Design:** Jörmungandr's job in surrounding the world mirrors the significance of keeping up with the equilibrium and construction of the universe. Its presence adds to the infinite request.

2. **Double Nature:** Jörmungandr's double nature features the complicated transaction of powers known to mankind, where creation and obliteration are interconnected.

V. Moral and Philosophical Ramifications

The presence of creature gods in creation fantasies conveys moral and philosophical ramifications, offering bits of knowledge into human points of view on the idea of presence and the equilibrium of enormous powers.

Moral Illustrations

Creation legends highlighting creature divinities frequently convey moral illustrations about the significance of equilibrium, overflow, and the interconnectedness of all living things. These illustrations accentuate the requirement for capable stewardship of the Earth.

Philosophical Reflections

Creature divinities welcome philosophical examination about the idea of the universe, the powers that shape it, and the exchange of creation and annihilation. They challenge people to consider their spot in the universe and the moral obligations that emerge from it.

VI. Difficulties and Contemporary Understandings

The meaning of creature gods in creation legends faces difficulties and transformations in the cutting edge world. As societies advance and profound viewpoints change, the pertinence of these legends keeps on being reworked and reconsidered.

Social Allocation

The allocation of creature gods and their imagery in business and well known settings has raised worries about social responsiveness and regard for the practices from which these fantasies begin. It is fundamental for people to move toward these fantasies with a comprehension of their social and profound legacy.

Ecological Mindfulness

The association between creature divinities and the regular world highlights the significance of protection endeavors. Many societies that adore these animals are effectively associated with protecting the climate and its biodiversity.

Contemporary Transformations

Creature divinities keep on moving contemporary craftsmanship, writing, and narrating. Their imagery stays pertinent with regards to present day translations, adding to continuous conversations about the powers that shape the universe and our job inside it.

3.3 Origin Stories and Animal Archetypes

Histories and creature originals have been woven into the texture of human culture since days of yore. These stories act as a basic structure for grasping the world, our place in it, and the multifaceted associations among people and the normal world. In this paper, we will investigate the significant meaning of histories and dive into the getting through presence of creature originals in human narrating.

1. **The Meaning of Histories**
1. **Social Personality and Having a place**
   Histories structure the bedrock of social personality, offering networks a common story that ties them together. These stories make sense of the production of the world, the rise of mankind, and the qualities that support a specific culture. For instance, in Native Australian Dreamtime stories, the land, its elements, and the animals that possess it are unpredictably associated, mirroring a significant feeling of having a place with the regular world.
2. **Feeling of Direction and Importance**
   Histories furnish people with a feeling of direction and importance, responding to existential inquiries concerning human life. They offer clarifications for the intricacies of life, demise, enduring, and the secrets of the universe. For example, the Beginning story in the Judeo-Christian custom clarifies the motivation behind human life and the outcomes of moral decisions.
3. **Moral and Moral Systems**

These accounts frequently act as moral and moral compasses, conferring illustrations spot on and wrong way of behaving. Through the hardships of characters in histories, social orders convey their qualities and standards. The Aesop's tales, for instance, use humanized creatures to grant moral illustrations, exhibiting the getting through force of these accounts in molding moral structures.

II. Creature Models in Human Narrating

1. **The Imagery of Creatures**
   Creatures have for some time been strong images in human narrating, addressing a large number of characteristics, ways of behaving, and qualities. For example, the shrewdness and creativity of the fox, the strength and boldness of the lion, and the insight of the owl all act as prototype portrayals profoundly imbued in our shared mindset.
2. **Social Varieties in Creature Models**
   Various societies credit novel implications to creatures, bringing about a rich embroidery of original portrayals. In Chinese culture, the winged serpent represents influence, strength, and favorable luck, while in Local American practices, the bear epitomizes characteristics of solidarity, reflection, and change. These varieties feature the comprehensiveness of the paradigm while stressing the social subtleties that shape its understanding.
3. **Mental and Profound Reverberation**

Creature originals tap into well established mental and close to home reactions inside people. They act as mirrors through which people can consider their own assets, shortcomings, and desires. The tale of the turtle and the rabbit, for instance, resounds with our inborn comprehension of steadiness and tolerance as excellencies.

III. The Development of Creature Originals

1. **Transformation and Syncretism**
   Creature prime examples have exhibited astounding flexibility, developing close by human social orders. As societies experience new conditions, convictions, and impacts, these prime examples syncretize and change, bringing about hybridized structures that mirror the powerful idea of human narrating. The juxtaposition of the Western idea of the unicorn with the Eastern kirin represents this versatility.

2. **Current Understandings and Pertinence**

In contemporary narrating, creature paradigms keep on assuming a critical part, frequently utilized to convey complex subjects and thoughts. From writing and film to promoting and marking, these originals proceed to dazzle and resound with crowds. The persevering through prominence of characters like Mowgli from "The Wilderness Book" or Simba from "The Lion Lord" bears witness to the getting through allure of creature paradigms in current culture.

Chapter 4

Metaphorical Menageries: Animals as Symbols

Creatures have assumed a significant and persevering through part in human culture, writing, craftsmanship, religion, and daily existence as images. This broad and different allegorical zoo has developed over hundreds of years, with various societies ascribing unmistakable implications and attributes to different creatures. In this exposition, we will investigate the complex snare of images related with creatures, revealing insight into how these illustrations have formed human comprehension and articulation.

1. **The Universality of Creature Images**
1. **Diverse Importance**
   The utilization of creatures as images is a worldwide peculiarity, rising above geological and social limits. From the old Egyptian respect for the feline as an image of beauty and insurance to the Chinese zodiac's attribution of character qualities to creatures, these images reverberate with individuals across various social orders.
2. **Authentic and Legendary Roots**
   Creature images frequently have their starting points in old legends, strict texts, and old stories. For instance, the scriptural snake is an image of enticement and crafty, while the Greek Sphinx addresses puzzler and secret. These old stories and convictions have left an enduring engraving on the aggregate human cognizance.
3. **Contemporary Pertinence**

In contemporary society, creature images keep on holding critical importance. They show up in writing, workmanship, publicizing, marking, and, surprisingly, political talk. Famous logos, for example, the Nike Swoosh or the Twitter bird outline the getting through force of creature images in current correspondence and promoting.

II. The Changed Imagery of Creatures

1. Strength and Fortitude

Certain creatures, similar to the lion, are frequently connected with strength and fortitude. In different societies, the lion is an image of dauntlessness and sovereignty. The lion's depiction as a wild and respectable animal can be followed back to old civilizations like Egypt and Mesopotamia.

2. Intelligence and Information

Owls are regularly portrayed as images of intelligence and information. The owl's relationship with astuteness can be followed to old Greek folklore, where it was connected to the goddess Athena, the encapsulation of intelligence. This persevering through image is as yet present in contemporary schooling and writing.

3. Flexibility and Change

The butterfly is an image of change and flexibility. Its life cycle, from a caterpillar to a chrysalis lastly to a butterfly, is viewed as an illustration for self-improvement and change. This imagery is especially critical in different societies and self improvement writing.

4. Guile and Trickiness

The fox is a general image of shrewd and slyness. In Aesop's tales, the fox frequently outsmarts different creatures through shrewdness and duplicity, embodying its getting through prime example as a tricky and cunning person.

5. Security and Guardianship

Creatures can likewise represent security and guardianship. The old Egyptians venerated the scarab bug as an image of security and resurrection. In many societies, canines are viewed as faithful defenders and are frequently connected with steadfastness and loyalty.

III. Social Varieties in Creature Imagery

1. Chinese Zodiac

The Chinese zodiac is a conspicuous illustration of the social variety in creature imagery. Every year is related with a particular creature sign, and individuals brought into the world in that year are accepted to acquire the qualities of that creature. This framework mirrors the significant job of creatures in Chinese culture, attributing characteristics like knowledge, dedication, and appeal to different animals.

2. Local American Soul Creatures

Local American societies have their own rich embroidered artwork of creature imagery, frequently connected to the idea of soul creatures. Various creatures are accepted to give direction and insurance to people. The wolf, for example, addresses knowledge, authority, and strength, while the bear represents contemplation and change.

3. **Hinduism and Creature Divinities**

Hinduism, a religion with a profound association with creatures, highlights different divinities related with creature imagery. The elephant-headed god Ganesha addresses shrewdness and keenness, while the monkey god Hanuman encapsulates dedication and boldness. These creature gods assume essential parts in Hindu folklore and ceremonies.

IV. Mental and Close to home Reverberation

Creature images tap into well established mental and close to home reactions inside people. They frequently act as mirrors through which people can investigate and communicate their own sentiments, wants, and fears. The picture of an independent person, for instance, resounds with how we might interpret freedom and confidence, while the pigeon represents harmony and concordance.

V. Advancement of Creature Images

1. **Variation and Syncretism**

   Creature images, similar to every social component, adjust and develop over the long haul. As social orders change and interface, these images syncretize and change, leading to new understandings. For instance, the winged serpent, an image of influence and favorable luck in Chinese culture, has taken on various implications in Western folklore.

2. **Contemporary Reevaluations**

In present day writing, workmanship, and mainstream society, creature images keep on being reconsidered. George Orwell's "Animal Homestead" utilizes human creatures to ridicule political philosophies, while the film "Life of Pi" investigates subjects of endurance and otherworldliness through a kid's excursion with a Bengal tiger.

VI. Moral Contemplations

While creature images enhance human culture, taking into account the moral ramifications of involving creatures as metaphors is critical. In this present reality where untamed life is under danger and creature double-dealing is a developing concern, the commodification of creature images brings up moral issues. How might we mindfully celebrate and utilize these images without propagating damage to real creatures?

4.1 Animals as Representations of Virtues and Vices

From the beginning of time, creatures have been utilized as strong images to address temperances and indecencies in human culture. These emblematic affiliations have given us a rich embroidery of similitudes that offer experiences into human instinct, ethical quality, and the perplexing exchange among great and fiendishness. In this exposition, we will investigate how creatures have come to exemplify different excellencies and indecencies, enlightening the manners by which these representations have impacted how we might interpret human person and conduct.

1. **Ideals Typified by Creatures**
1. **Dedication and Steadfastness**
   The idea of dedication and steadfastness has for some time been addressed by creatures, with canines being the most unmistakable model. Canines have procured their standing as steadfast friends, mirroring the excellence of resolute loyalty. Accounts of canines hanging tight for their proprietors, even after their proprietors have died, embody the profundity of this security and the devotion it represents.
2. **Intelligence and Information**
   Owls, frequently seen as images of shrewdness, have held an exceptional spot in human culture. This affiliation can be followed back to antiquated Greek folklore, where the owl was connected to the goddess Athena, who addressed astuteness. The owl's apparent insight is reflected in its quiet disposition and full concentrations eyes, making it an immortal portrayal of cleverness.
3. **Mental fortitude and Strength**
   Creatures like lions and hawks are frequently connected with boldness and strength. The lion, with its majestic mane and furious disposition, has been an image of boldness and respectability in different societies. Essentially, the bird, with its strong claws and sharp visual perception, addresses strength and valiance. These creatures summon a feeling of determination and courage.
4. **Tolerance and Tirelessness**

The turtle, an animal known for its gradual advancement, has turned into an image of tolerance and tirelessness. Aesop's tale of "The Turtle and the Bunny" features the worth of diligence over scurry, advancing the excellence of consistent assurance.

II. Indecencies Exemplified by Creatures

1. **Misleading and Duplicity**
   Creatures, for example, the fox and the snake are frequently connected with misleading and duplicity. The fox, known for its shrewdness and trickiness, is an exemplary image of trickery. In different tales and fables, the fox outmaneuvers different creatures through smart strategies. Also, the snake's job in scriptural stories, like enticing Eve in the Nursery of Eden, makes it a persevering through image of misdirection and allurement.
2. **Ravenousness and Abundance**
   Pigs are frequently used to represent ravenousness and abundance. Their unquenchable hunger and propensity to enjoy food make them a fitting portrayal

of extravagance. In writing and craftsmanship, the pig is in some cases portrayed as an image of overabundance, ravenousness, and moral corruption.

3. **Sloth and Apathy**

   The sloth, a sluggish and dormant animal, has come to represent sloth and lethargy. This affiliation is established in the creature's stationary way of life and conscious absence of action. Portrayals of the sloth frequently act as a wake up call of the bad habit of inertia and detachment.

4. **Malevolence and Animosity**

Snakes and snakes are often connected with vindictiveness and hostility. Their venomous nibbles and subtle developments have added to their depiction as images of vindictiveness. In many societies, the snake addresses risk, unfairness, and aggression.

III. Multifaceted Importance

The representative relationship of creatures with ideals and indecencies have risen above social limits, reflecting widespread subjects in human instinct. For instance, the idea of the honorable lion as an image of boldness and fearlessness is tracked down in different societies, from the African savannas to European heraldry.

Likewise, the snake as an image of trickery and enticement shows up in different legends and strict customs, from the scriptural story of the Nursery of Eden to the Nāga in Hinduism and Buddhism. These culturally diverse equals show the persevering through force of creature illustrations in conveying complex moral and moral ideas.

IV. Mental and Profound Reverberation

Creature images tap into firmly established mental and profound reactions inside people. They frequently act as mirrors through which people can investigate and communicate their own ideals and indecencies.

For instance, when we experience the picture of a devoted canine, it reverberates with our natural comprehension of unwaveringness and steadfastness as ethics. On the other hand, the picture of a guile fox might inspire reflections on misleading and cunning as indecencies.

V. Moral Contemplations

While creature images improve how we might interpret temperances and indecencies, taking into account the moral ramifications of these associations is fundamental. The utilization of creatures to address indecencies, like sloth and voracity, can coincidentally sustain negative generalizations about specific species. Moral contemplations likewise reach out to how creatures are dealt with and taken advantage of in different social practices and businesses.

VI. Contemporary Importance

Creature images keep on assuming a huge part in contemporary narrating, craftsmanship, promoting, and marking. In writing, characters roused by these creature illustrations frequently wrestle with temperances and indecencies, furnishing perusers with appealing moral situations. In promoting, creature images are utilized to pass on brand values and messages, building up the persevering through force of these illustrations in forming shopper discernments.

4.2 Cultural Variations in Symbolism

Images are a fundamental piece of human correspondence and articulation. They act as a scaffold between the unmistakable and the elusive, permitting us to convey complex thoughts, feelings, and ideas through a visual, hear-able, or even material structure. Be that as it may, the significance and understanding of images are not widespread yet are intensely impacted by social varieties. These social varieties in imagery assume a vital part in molding our view of the world, our character, and the manner in which we collaborate with others. In this article, we will investigate the rich and various universe of social varieties in imagery, digging into how various societies appoint importance to images, their verifiable and humanistic setting, and the effect of globalization on the advancement of representative language.

The Idea of Images

Images are a major part of human perception. They are not restricted to a particular medium or frame and can take the state of words, pictures, signals, customs, and even items. An image is basically a portrayal that represents something past its exacting importance.

For instance, a red rose can represent love, a heart might address friendship, and a cross frequently implies Christianity. Images are a method for conveying meaning and impart complex thoughts productively, making them a foundation of culture and correspondence.

Social varieties in imagery emerge from the way that images are not intrinsically significant. They gain their importance through shared social encounters and setting. What one culture considers as an image of favorable luck may be viewed as a sign of misfortune in another. In this manner, the understanding of images fluctuates across societies and even inside subcultures.

Authentic Underlying foundations of Social Images

The authentic underlying foundations of social images are profoundly interwoven with the improvement of social orders and their qualities. The utilization of images to address dynamic ideas or to send information is old, tracing all the way back to ancient times. Cave compositions, for instance, are one of the earliest types of emblematic correspondence, filling in as a way to portray hunting scenes, strict customs, and social stories.

Generally speaking, images have their starting points in strict or otherworldly convictions. The cross, for example, is a critical image in Christianity, addressing the torturous killing of Jesus Christ and his ensuing revival. This image holds profound strict and social importance inside Christian people group. Essentially, the Om image in Hinduism represents the pith of a definitive reality, cognizance, and godliness.

These images have persevered for quite a long time and keep on being powerful in the existences of individuals who stick to these beliefs.

Humanistic Setting of Images

Social images are not simply erratic portrayals; they are profoundly implanted in the social texture of a local area. They mirror the qualities, standards, and convictions of a general public and assist with keeping up with social union. Images can support character, lay out limits, and advance a feeling of having a place among people in a specific culture.

Banners are fantastic instances of images that serve humanistic capabilities. They address countries and, likewise, individuals and standards related with those countries. The American banner, with its stars and stripes, addresses not just the US as a political substance yet additionally the common character and upsides of its residents. Consuming or defiling a public banner is much of the time thought about a strong demonstration of dissent, exhibiting the representative significance of banners in social orders.

Additionally, images can likewise act as devices of avoidance. At times, images are utilized to recognize insiders from untouchables or to flag one's connection with a specific gathering. For example, pack related images or tattoos are utilized to convey devotion and personality inside subcultures, however they likewise act as an advance notice or challenge to outcasts.

The Impact of Globalization

Globalization significantly affects social images. With the rising interconnectedness of the world through innovation, exchange, and travel, societies are associating like never before previously. This cooperation has prompted the dissemination and reevaluation of images across borders, now and again obscuring the lines between societies.

One manner by which globalization has impacted images is through the spread of mainstream society. The images and symbols of worldwide diversion, like Hollywood movies, K-popular music, or Japanese anime, have tracked down crowds a long ways past their nations of beginning. Accordingly, images related with these social items can be perceived and deciphered in different regions of the planet. For instance, the gesture of goodwill, promoted during the nonconformity development of the 1960s in the US, has turned into a widespread image for harmony and love.

Then again, globalization has likewise prompted the commodification and at times assignment of social images. Customary images or practices are frequently repackaged and promoted to a worldwide crowd, here and there stripping them of their unique importance. The act of yoga, for example, has been popularized and worked on in numerous Western nations, separating it from its otherworldly and social roots in India.

The Advancement of Images

Social images are not static yet develop over the long run in light of changing cultural qualities, convictions, and standards. As societies adjust to new conditions, images can take on new implications or translations, mirroring the developing idea of human social orders.

Language and imagery are firmly related, and changes in language can impact the importance of images. For instance, the LGBTQ+ pride banner, with its rainbow tones, has advanced to incorporate extra tones and varieties to all the more likely address the variety of sexual directions and orientation characters. This development of the banner's imagery lines up with the developing acknowledgment of the intricacy of human sexuality and orientation.

Political developments can likewise impact the advancement of images. The People of color Matter development presented the raised clench hand as an image of obstruction and fortitude. This image, with its authentic roots in social equality activism, has taken on new importance with regards to contemporary civil rights developments.

Difficulties and Discussions

Social images can be a wellspring of pride and solidarity, however they can likewise be a reason for struggle and misconstruing. Contentions frequently emerge when images are deciphered contrastingly or when one culture embraces the images of one more without appropriate comprehension or regard.

Social allocation is a huge issue in this specific circumstance. At the point when components of one culture are acquired or taken by one more culture without authorization or understanding, it can prompt offense and social obtuseness. For instance, the wearing of Local American crowns by non-Local people as style proclamations has been broadly censured as a type of social assignment, as these hats hold profound otherworldly and social importance for Local American people group.

Strict images, as well, can be a wellspring of strain and struggle. The utilization of strict images out in the open spaces, like schools or government structures, can be a combative issue, as it very well might be viewed as a support of one religion over others or as an infringement of the standard of division of chapel and state. These discussions feature the complicated exchange between social images, opportunity of articulation, and strict variety.

Social images can likewise be controlled for political purposes. Political pioneers might utilize images to energize support, advance patriotism, or redirect consideration from major problems. This control of images can prompt the bending of their unique implications and can add to the polarization of social orders.

4.3 The Universal Language of Animal Metaphors

Illustrations are a principal part of human language and discernment, permitting us to convey dynamic ideas and thoughts by drawing matches with concrete, substantial encounters. From the beginning of time, one class of illustrations has reliably arisen as a widespread and multifaceted device for correspondence and articulation: creature similitudes. These representations draw upon the attributes, ways of behaving, and imagery of creatures to help us comprehend and convey different parts of the human experience. This exposition investigates the widespread language of creature analogies, their beginnings, social varieties, and the manners in which they improve how we might interpret the world.

The Omnipresence of Creature Similitudes

Creature allegories are ubiquitous in language and thought across societies. They act as a scaffold between the human and creature universes, empowering us to portray complex feelings, ways of behaving, and circumstances in an engaging and distinctive way. This comprehensiveness can be seen in the colloquial articulations, axioms, and allegories that draw upon creature credits and ways of behaving to convey meaning. From "smart as a whip" to "obstinate as a donkey," creatures are woven into the texture of our phonetic and mental systems.

The Allure of Creature Analogies

The broad utilization of creature illustrations can be credited to a few variables. First and foremost, creatures are generally perceived and experienced by people, no matter what their social or semantic foundations. This common knowledge of creatures makes creature similitudes effectively available and fathomable. Furthermore, creatures encapsulate a great many ways of behaving, qualities, and imagery, which can be adjusted to convey different parts of human instinct and the human experience. For instance, a lion might address strength and boldness, while a snake might represent misleading and risk.

The all inclusiveness of creature representations additionally connects with the well established association among people and the regular world. All through our transformative history, we have shared spaces, assets, and connections with creatures. This cozy relationship has given sufficient chances to people to notice and gain from creatures, prompting the improvement of figurative language established in the animals of the world collectively.

Beginnings of Creature Illustrations

Creature similitudes have old starting points, tracing all the way back to the earliest human civic establishments. The utilization of creatures in similitudes and imagery is firmly connected to the rise of human culture and the improvement of language. In many societies, creatures were worshipped and integrated into strict and fanciful accounts, further solidifying their importance as allegorical images.

In antiquated Egypt, for example, different creatures like the feline, hawk, and jackal were related with various gods and held emblematic worth. The idea of Ma'at, frequently addressed as a plume, represented equilibrium and request and was related with the ostrich feather.

In the Western practice, the lion has been an image of solidarity and honorability since old Greece. The Nemean lion, a legendary animal, was one of the twelve works of Heracles (Hercules). This imagery reached out to the Medieval times when the lion was utilized as an image of eminence and power.

Likewise, creatures play played critical parts in Eastern societies. The Chinese zodiac, for example, comprises of twelve creature signs, each related with specific character qualities and ways of behaving. These creatures are regularly utilized in Chinese representations and imagery.

Social Varieties in Creature Allegories

While creature allegories are general, they are not uniform. Various societies might decipher and utilize creature representations in extraordinary ways, mirroring their own qualities, convictions, and encounters. These social varieties add profundity and subtlety to the general language of creature representations.

Chinese Culture: The Chinese zodiac, referenced prior, is a great representation of how creatures are utilized figuratively to portray character qualities and life altering situations. Individuals brought into the world in the Time of the Rodent, for instance, are frequently connected with keenness and genius, while those brought into the world in the Extended period of the Bull are viewed as dedicated and solid. These creature representations are profoundly imbued in Chinese culture and impact different parts of life, from picking a marriage accomplice to settling on significant life choices.

Local American Customs: Numerous Local American clans have creature emblems and soul creatures that are fundamental to their profound convictions and figurative language. Every creature addresses explicit characteristics and lessons. The bear, for example, is frequently connected with strength and thoughtfulness, while the wolf represents family and local area.

African Sayings: African societies have a rich custom of involving creature representations in precepts and narrating. These illustrations are frequently utilized to grant insight and life examples. For example, the Swahili precept "Haraka, haraka haina baraka" (Rush, hustle has no gifts) utilizes the representation of a turtle to alert against eagerness.

Native Dreamtime: In Australian Native culture, the Dreamtime, or the Dreaming, is a period of creation when genealogical creatures formed the land and its occupants. Numerous Dreamtime stories include creatures, and these creatures act as similitudes for the regular and otherworldly world. The kangaroo, for instance, is an image of perseverance and dexterity.

Norse Folklore: In Norse folklore, creatures assume huge parts as allegories and images. The wolf Fenrir addresses disorder and annihilation, while the snake Jörmungandr represents the steady battle against looming destruction. These analogies mirror the cruel and erratic nature of the Northern European scene and its kin.

In every one of these social settings, creature analogies give novel bits of knowledge into the qualities, convictions, and encounters of individuals. They offer a window into the manner in which various societies comprehend and decipher their general surroundings, featuring the rich variety of human idea and articulation.

The Social Meaning of Creature Allegories

Creature allegories fill different needs inside societies, frequently reflecting and building up social qualities and standards. Here are a portion of the vital jobs of creature illustrations in various social orders:

Social Character: Creature representations can be strong images of social personality. They assist with recognizing one culture from another and can be a wellspring of pride and solidarity. For instance, the falcon is an image of opportunity and public personality in the US.

Moral and Moral Direction: Creature analogies are frequently used to confer moral and moral illustrations. Tales and stories including creatures with unmistakable qualities and ways of behaving assist with conveying values and standards inside a general public. The Aesop's tale of "The Turtle and the Bunny" represents the significance of constancy and lowliness.

Customs and Services: Creatures might assume a focal part in social ceremonies and functions. In certain societies, the penance of creatures is a method for speaking with the profound domain or to look for security and endowments. In Hinduism, for instance, the cow is thought of as consecrated, and its milk and ghee (explained spread) are utilized in strict services.

Social Correspondence: Creature similitudes are a method for correspondence that rises above language hindrances. They permit individuals to communicate complex thoughts and feelings in manners that are effortlessly perceived by others. For instance, the Japanese idea of "tsundoku" alludes to the propensity for getting books and allowing them to stack up, uninitiated. It very well may be figuratively portrayed as "having a book zoo."

Relational Connections: Creature analogies are frequently used to depict human characters and connections. Individuals may be portrayed as "smart as a whip" or "totally silent." These illustrations give a compact approach to conveying character qualities and ways of behaving.

Influence on Writing and Workmanship

Creature illustrations significantly affect writing and workmanship since forever ago. They act as a wellspring of motivation for narrating, verse, and visual expressions. A portion of the world's most renowned works of writing and workmanship attract upon creature representations to convey complex thoughts and feelings.

Writing:

George Orwell's "Animal Ranch" is a strong moral story that utilizes a cast of livestock to address various parts of human culture and legislative issues, like despotism and the maltreatment of force.

Aesop's tales, an assortment of brief tales including creatures as characters, give moral examples that have persevered for a really long time.

Franz Kafka's "Transformation" recounts the tale of an up limited morning to end up changed into a goliath bug, utilizing the illustration of the bug to investigate subjects of distance and personality.

Workmanship:

Hieronymus Bosch's "The Nursery of Natural Enjoyments" includes a wide cluster of creature imagery to portray humankind's corrupt and decadent nature.

Leonardo da Vinci's "Investigation of Feline Developments and Positions" exhibits his interest with life systems and the mechanics of development, involving the feline as a subject for logical investigation.

These models outline how creature representations have enhanced human imagination and imaginative articulation, giving an extraordinary focal point through which to investigate and grasp the human condition.

The Moral Component of Creature Similitudes

While creature representations are a strong and generally involved device for correspondence and articulation, they likewise bring up moral issues. How creatures are depicted in allegories can impact our view of them and, at times, sustain generalizations or destructive convictions.

For example, typical statements like "hungry Harry" and "hard as a worker" suggest that these creatures are energetically enterprising. While these similitudes are by and large utilized in a positive light, they can propagate the conviction that creatures exist exclusively for human double-dealing or that their worth depends on their efficiency.

Also, pessimistic generalizations related with specific creatures, like the trickery of foxes or the weakness of mice, can sustain incorrect and unjustifiable convictions about both the creatures and individuals to whom these illustrations are applied.

Besides, a few creature representations might minimize or downplay difficult issues connected with creature government assistance and preservation. Phrases like "solve two problems at once" or "beat a dead pony" may incidentally reduce the significance of moral treatment of creaturesConsidering these contemplations, it is vital to utilize creature allegories with awareness and care, taking into account their likely effect on the manner in which we see and cooperate with the normal world.

Chapter 5

Beasts in Divine Guise: Anthropomorphic Deities

Human divinities, divine beings and goddesses that expect human-like structures, are a typical element in numerous strict and fanciful practices around the world. These divinities frequently exemplify a mix of human and creature qualities, leading to the interesting idea of humanoid attribution. This exposition digs into the universe of human divinities with an emphasis on those that integrate creature credits into their heavenly personas. It investigates the starting points, social importance, and emblematic implications of these divinities across various societies, uncovering the diverse idea of these perplexing and interesting heavenly creatures.

Starting points of Human Divinities

The idea of humanoid attribution with regards to gods can be followed back to the earliest human civilizations and their collaborations with the normal world. In ancient times, people frequently tried to make sense of and get a handle on the regular powers and animals that encompassed them. This prompted the making of fanciful stories and the introduction of human gods.

Antiquated Egypt: One of the most notable instances of human gods can be tracked down in old Egyptian folklore. The divine beings and goddesses of antiquated Egypt frequently showed human-like bodies with creature heads. For example, the god Thoth was portrayed with the top of an ibis, while the goddess Bastet had the top of a lioness. These divinities addressed different parts of life and the normal world, and their mixture structures represented the interconnectedness of people and creatures in the Egyptian cosmology.

Mesopotamia: In the old human advancements of Mesopotamia, for example, Sumer and Babylon, human gods were additionally common. The god Enki, related with water, had the lower body of a fish. Likewise, the goddess Ishtar, addressing affection and richness, was frequently portrayed with the wings of a bird. These half breed structures were emblematic of the gods' territory over unambiguous domains, interfacing them to the creature and regular universes.

Hinduism: Hinduism, one of the world's most seasoned religions, includes a rich pantheon of human gods. For example, Ruler Ganesha, the elephant-headed god, is the remover of impediments and the supporter of acumen and insight. His novel structure, conceived out of an entrancing legendary story, addresses the heavenly union of human and creature credits. Essentially, Ruler Hanuman, a monkey-confronted divinity, epitomizes characteristics of solidarity, dedication, and unwaveringness.

Greek Folklore: Greek folklore is packed with human divinities, including the Olympian divine beings and goddesses who displayed both human and creature credits. Container, the lord of the wild, had the legs and horns of a goat, mirroring his association with nature. Artemis, the goddess of the chase, was frequently portrayed with deer prongs on her head, highlighting her job as a defender of natural life.

Social Meaning of Human Gods

The presence of human gods in different societies conveys significant social and otherworldly importance. These gods fill a large number of needs, mirroring the qualities, convictions, and perspectives of their particular societies.

Spanning the Human-Creature Separation: Human divinities frequently act as a scaffold between the human and creature universes. They encapsulate the possibility that people are interconnected with the regular world, mirroring a love for the climate and the animals that possess it. In many societies, these gods accentuate the significance of regarding and existing together with the collective of animals.

Imagery and Moral story: Human divinities often address further emblematic implications. Their half and half structures might epitomize characteristics or traits related with the creature they look like. For instance, the goddess Bastet's lioness head represented her job as a defender and nurturer, while likewise addressing the furious and defensive parts of parenthood.

Watchmen and Middle people: In certain societies, human gods act as gatekeepers and arbiters among people and the heavenly. These divinities are accepted to have a special comprehension of both the human and creature domains, making them ideal defenders and middle people in issues connected with horticulture, richness, and the prosperity of the local area.

Social Personality: The presence of human divinities frequently builds up a culture's special character and perspective. These gods become an indispensable piece of a culture's strict and fanciful stories, impacting its specialty, ceremonies, and customs.

Representative Implications of Creature Credits

Creature ascribes inside human divinities convey rich emblematic implications that add profundity to the comprehension of these heavenly creatures. A few normal representative understandings of creature credits include:

Strength and Power: Numerous creature credits, like the lion's mane or the bull's horns, represent strength and power. Gods with these characteristics frequently address characteristics like fortitude, predominance, and authority.

Shrewdness and Information: Creatures related with intelligence and information, like owls or snakes, can represent the divinity's job as a wellspring of direction and keenness. The owl, for example, is frequently connected to astuteness and premonition.

Effortlessness and Style: Creatures known for their effortlessness and class, similar to the swan or the gazelle, may connote the divinity's job as a benefactor of magnificence, craftsmanship, and refinement.

Ripeness and Overflow: Numerous creature credits, like the bull's relationship with richness, address the god's part in guaranteeing overflow, flourishing, and the progression of life.

Guardianship and Insurance: Gods with creature credits frequently act as gatekeepers and defenders. The creature types of these gods might represent their job as careful sentinels, safeguarding their enthusiasts from hurt.

Social Varieties in Human Gods

Various societies have their special translations of human divinities with creature credits, each offering a particular viewpoint on the connection between people, creatures, and the heavenly. The following are a couple of models:

Old Egyptian Divinities: In old Egypt, the lioness-headed goddess Bastet addressed home, fruitfulness, and labor. She was many times portrayed as a sustaining and defensive god, underscoring the significance of homegrown life and the prosperity of the family.

Hindu Gods: Hinduism includes a wide cluster of human divinities with creature credits. Master Ganesha, the elephant-headed god, is commended as the remover of hindrances and the supplier of intelligence. His picture is frequently conjured toward the start of huge endeavors to guarantee a positive outcome and security.

Antiquated Greek Divinities: The Greek goddess Artemis, frequently connected with the chase and wild, was represented by the presence of deer tusks on her head. These prongs addressed her association with nature and the job she played as a defender of nature.

Local American Otherworldliness: Numerous Local American clans have their extraordinary pantheon of human gods and soul creatures. The Navajo public, for example, love the Corn Lady, a god with properties of the two people and plants. She addresses the fundamental association between farming, the development of corn, and the prosperity of the local area.

Japanese Fables: In Japanese legends, the Kitsune, a shape-moving fox, is a conspicuous human divinity. Kitsune are accepted to have insight, shrewdness, and enchanted abilities, filling in as middle people among people and the otherworldly domain.

The getting through presence of human divinities with creature ascribes across these different societies highlights the comprehensiveness of the human interest with the regular world and the intricate connection among people and creatures.

Imaginative Articulations of Human Gods

Imaginative portrayals of human gods play had a critical impact in conveying their social and emblematic implications. These portrayals take different structures, including figures, works of art, and ceremonies, and they frequently give a visual connection between the human and heavenly domains.

Sculptures and Figures: Many societies have made complicated sculptures and models of their human divinities, catching their interesting ascribes and characteristics. These imaginative portrayals act as actual exemplifications of the divinities and are in many cases set in sanctuaries, holy places, and hallowed spaces.

Compositions and Iconography: The utilization of works of art and iconography has permitted specialists to portray human divinities in different structures and settings. These pictures are much of the time utilized in strict customs, stories, and as helps in reflection and supplication.

Customs and Functions: Human divinities are oftentimes summoned in strict customs and services. In Hinduism, for instance, symbols of divinities like Master Ganesha and Ruler Hanuman are key to numerous strict functions and celebrations. These ceremonies act for of associating with the heavenly presence of these gods.

Narrating and Folklore: Accounts and anecdotes about human divinities with creature ascribes are in many cases gone down through oral customs, composed texts, and legendary stories. These accounts assist with conveying the social importance and representative implications of these gods to people in the future.

The Impact of Human Gods on Human Culture

Human divinities have affected human culture in different ways, molding social, strict, and creative articulations:

Moral and Moral Qualities: The narratives and characteristics of human gods frequently contain moral and moral lessons that guide the way of behaving and upsides of a culture. For example, the traits of insight and knowledge related with specific divinities might support characteristics like information chasing and reasonability.

Craftsmanship and Style: The imaginative portrayals of human gods have propelled innumerable show-stoppers, impacting engineering, model, painting, and different types of innovative articulation. These divinities act as dreams and images of excellence and beauty in craftsmanship.

Ceremonies and Customs: Human divinities assume a focal part in strict customs and customs. These ceremonies act for of love, supplication, and association with the heavenly, encouraging a feeling of otherworldliness and local area among fans.

Social Personality: Human gods are frequently symbolic of a culture's character, forming its strict and fanciful stories. The presence of these divinities builds up a culture's special perspective and values.

Ecological Mindfulness: The adoration for human divinities with creature credits frequently stretches out to the regular world. These gods highlight the interconnectedness among people and the climate, advancing ecological awareness and stewardship.

5.1 Gods and Goddesses with Animal Attributes

All through mankind's set of experiences, divine beings and goddesses have been a focal piece of strict and fanciful customs across the world. Large numbers of these heavenly creatures are described by their interesting credits, which frequently incorporate a mix of human and creature highlights. These divine beings and goddesses with creature credits possess a critical spot in the pantheon of different societies, representing the association among people and the regular world.

This exposition dives into the interesting domain of divine beings and goddesses with creature ascribes, investigating their starting points, social importance, and the imagery they convey.

Beginnings of Divine beings and Goddesses with Creature Ascribes

The idea of divine beings and goddesses with creature ascribes has old starting points, tracing all the way back to the earliest human civic establishments. These heavenly creatures frequently arose as a method for making sense of normal peculiarities, human qualities, and the secrets of the world. The starting points of such divinities can be followed to different sources:

Nature Love: In numerous early social orders, the love of regular components and creatures was common. People loved creatures for their solidarity, spryness, or other astounding characteristics. Over the long run, these adored creatures became related with holiness, bringing about divine beings and goddesses with creature ascribes.

Imagery and Humanoid attribution: Humanoid attribution, the attribution of human qualities to creatures or items, assumed an essential part in the production of such gods. As people tried to get a handle on their general surroundings, they frequently extended their own characteristics onto creatures, prompting the idea of heavenly creatures that consolidated human and creature highlights.

Otherworldly and Strict Encounters: Many societies had faith in the profound and supernatural characteristics of creatures. Profound encounters, dreams, and dreams were frequently deciphered as experiences with divine creatures, every now and again assuming the type of creatures.

Legends and Accounts: The legendary stories of different societies frequently include divine beings and goddesses with creature ascribes. These legends gave clarifications to the making of the world, the starting points of people, and the powers overseeing the universe.

Social Meaning of Divine beings and Goddesses with Creature Ascribes

Divine beings and goddesses with creature credits hold significant social importance in their particular social orders. Their jobs and traits frequently reflect the qualities, convictions, and perspectives of the way of life that worship them. The social meaning of these heavenly creatures can be grasped in more than one way:

Otherworldly and Moral Direction: These gods much of the time act as well-springs of profound and moral direction. They epitomize characteristics or ways of behaving related with the creatures they address, which are then viewed as highminded or hallowed. For instance, a divinity with the properties of a shrewd owl might represent the significance of information and intelligence.

Association with Nature: Divine beings and goddesses with creature ascribes underscore the interconnectedness of people and the normal world. They act as tokens of the significant association between the human domain and the animals of the world collectively, uplifting veneration and regard for nature.

Emblematic Portrayal: These heavenly creatures frequently represent explicit parts of life, like ripeness, strength, or inventiveness. They might be conjured in customs and services to look for endowments or help with these areas. For instance, a goddess with the properties of a cow might be related with fruitfulness and overflow.

Social Personality: Divine beings and goddesses with creature credits assume an essential part in forming a culture's strict and fanciful character. They add to the uniqueness of a culture's perspective and turned into a vital piece of its shared mindset.

Craftsmanship and Style: The creative portrayals of these heavenly creatures have propelled endless masterpieces. Their symbolism frequently tracks down articulation in design, figure, painting, and different types of imaginative articulation.

Imagery of Creature Ascribes

The creature credits of divine beings and goddesses convey rich emblematic implications, which add profundity to the comprehension of these heavenly creatures. Here are a few normal emblematic understandings of creature credits:

Strength and Power: Numerous divine beings and goddesses with creature ascribes represent strength and power. Creatures eminent for their actual ability, like lions or bulls, frequently address characteristics like boldness, strength, and authority.

Shrewdness and Information: Traits of creatures related with intelligence and information, like owls or snakes, can represent the divinity's job as a wellspring of direction and keenness. For instance, the owl, frequently connected with intelligence, addresses premonition and knowledge.

Richness and Overflow: Numerous gods with creature credits represent ripeness and overflow. The properties of creatures connected to reproduction, like cows or bunnies, address the god's job in guaranteeing the congruity of life and the wealth of assets.

Guardianship and Security: These heavenly creatures frequently act as defenders and gatekeepers. The creature types of these gods might represent their job as vigilant sentinels, safeguarding their lovers from damage and risk.

Change and Variation: A few divine beings and goddesses with creature credits address change and versatility. They encapsulate the possibility that change and advancement are fundamental parts of life and otherworldliness.

Social Varieties in Divine beings and Goddesses with Creature Ascribes

Divine beings and goddesses with creature ascribes shift incredibly across various societies, mirroring the variety of human convictions and customs. Here are a few instances of these heavenly creatures in different social settings:

Hindu Divinities: Hinduism includes a rich pantheon of divine beings and goddesses with creature credits. Master Ganesha, with the top of an elephant, is worshipped as the remover of impediments and the divinity of insight and shrewdness. His extraordinary structure addresses the combination of human and creature ascribes, representing his heavenly characteristics.

Egyptian Divinities: Old Egyptian folklore incorporates divine beings and goddesses with creature credits, for example, Bastet, who has the top of a lioness. Bastet is related with home, ripeness, and labor, exemplifying supporting characteristics. Also, the god Thoth, with the top of an ibis, addresses intelligence and information.

Greek Folklore: Greek folklore highlights divine beings and goddesses with creature credits, for example, Dish, the lord of the wild, who has the legs and horns of a goat. Container addresses the untamed and eccentric parts of nature. Artemis, the goddess of the chase, is frequently portrayed with deer tusks on her head, representing her job as a defender of natural life.

Aztec Divinities: In Aztec culture, the god Tezcatlipoca had the characteristics of a panther, meaning his association with the strange and perplexing powers of the evening. Tezcatlipoca encapsulated both disastrous and innovative angles, mirroring the double idea of presence.

Local American Otherworldliness: Numerous Local American clans have their own divine beings and goddesses with creature credits and soul creatures. The Corn Lady, a god with properties of the two people and plants, addresses the fundamental association between farming, corn development, and the prosperity of the local area.

These models exhibit the assorted manners by which divine beings and goddesses with creature credits are adored and deciphered in various societies. While the particular credits and jobs of these heavenly creatures might differ, the fundamental subject of interconnectedness among people and creatures stays a consistent idea.

Creative Articulations of Divine beings and Goddesses with Creature Ascribes

Imaginative portrayals of divine beings and goddesses with creature credits play had a huge impact in conveying their social and representative implications. These creative articulations take different structures, including figures, canvases, customs, and functions. They frequently give a visual connection between the human and heavenly domains and act as central focuses for commitment and profound association.

Sculptures and Figures: Many societies make unpredictable sculptures and models of divine beings and goddesses with creature credits. These portrayals catch the novel elements and characteristics of the divinities, making them open for love and reverence in sanctuaries, sanctums, and sacrosanct spaces.

Works of art and Iconography: The utilization of compositions and iconography permits specialists to portray these heavenly creatures in different structures and settings. These pictures are many times utilized in strict customs, stories, and as helps in reflection and supplication.

Customs and Services: Divine beings and goddesses with creature ascribes assume focal parts in strict customs and functions. These ceremonies give valuable open doors to lovers to interface with the heavenly presence of these divinities, look for favors, and deal love.

Narrating and Folklore: Accounts and anecdotes about these heavenly creatures are much of the time elapsed down through oral practices, composed texts, and legendary stories. These accounts assist with conveying the social importance and representative implications of the divine beings and goddesses to people in the future.

The Impact of Divine beings and Goddesses with Creature Ascribes on Human Culture

Divine beings and goddesses with creature credits have affected human culture in different ways, molding social, strict, and imaginative articulations. Their impact is apparent in:

Moral and Moral Qualities: The properties and accounts of these heavenly creatures frequently contain moral and moral lessons that guide the way of behaving and upsides of a culture. For instance, a god related with insight might empower characteristics like information chasing and reasonability.

Workmanship and Style: The creative portrayals of these divine beings and goddesses have roused endless masterpieces. Their symbolism frequently tracks down articulation in engineering, model, painting, and different types of imaginative articulation.

Ceremonies and Customs: These heavenly creatures assume essential parts in strict customs and customs, cultivating a feeling of otherworldliness and local area among lovers.

Social Character: Divine beings and goddesses with creature credits are symbolic of a culture's personality, molding its strict and fanciful stories. They add to the uniqueness of a culture's perspective and character.

Ecological Mindfulness: The respect for these heavenly creatures frequently reaches out to the regular world, accentuating the interconnectedness among people and the climate. This advances ecological awareness and stewardship.

5.2 The Concept of Zoomorphism

Zoomorphism is an interesting and old idea that includes crediting creature qualities or structures to non-creature elements, including gods, people, items, or theoretical thoughts. This idea is profoundly imbued in human culture and history, frequently filling in as an extension between the regular world and human culture. Zoomorphism assumes a critical part in craftsmanship, religion, writing, and folklore, offering bits of knowledge into the human comprehension of the collective of animals and its emblematic importance. This article investigates the idea of zoomorphism, its verifiable and social roots, and its different articulations across various parts of human civilization.

Starting points of Zoomorphism

The idea of zoomorphism is established in the human interest with the set of all animals and its assorted occupants. This interest traces all the way back to the earliest human social orders, where people firmly noticed and collaborated with creatures right at home. A few variables added to the starting points of zoomorphism:

Perception of Creature Conduct: Early people noticed the way of behaving of creatures and noticed their exceptional attributes, qualities, and capacities. These perceptions frequently enlivened deference and regard, prompting the attribution of creature characteristics to different substances.

Representative Importance: The ways of behaving and qualities of creatures frequently held emblematic significance. For instance, the strength of a lion or the insight of an owl should have been visible as characteristics to imitate or revere. Early social orders saw creatures as strong images that could convey more profound implications or examples.

Strict and Fanciful Impact: Numerous old religions and folklores included gods, spirits, and animals with creature ascribes. The divine beings and goddesses of different pantheons were frequently portrayed with creature heads, wings, or different highlights, meaning their association with the normal world and their jobs as delegates among people and the heavenly.

Social Customs: Zoomorphic imagery assumed a fundamental part in social practices, including totemism and shamanism. Numerous native societies overall had tribal creatures that addressed the group or clan's character and values. Shamans frequently conjured creature spirits to look for direction or mending.

Zoomorphism in Religion and Folklore

Zoomorphism is conspicuously highlighted in different strict and fanciful customs, where divine beings, spirits, and heavenly creatures frequently have creature credits or take on creature structures. These substances act as middle people between the human and heavenly domains and convey explicit representative implications.

Antiquated Egypt: In old Egyptian folklore, numerous divine beings and goddesses displayed human bodies with creature heads or other creature highlights. For example, the god Thoth, related with insight and information, had the top of an ibis. The goddess Bastet, addressing home, ripeness, and labor, was frequently portrayed with the top of a lioness. These divinities exemplified different parts of life and the normal world and underscored the interconnectedness of people and creatures in the Egyptian cosmology.

Hinduism: Hinduism includes a rich pantheon of divine beings and goddesses with creature credits. Ruler Ganesha, the elephant-headed god, is the remover of snags and the supporter of astuteness and shrewdness.

His special structure addresses the heavenly blend of human and creature credits and implies his part in eliminating hindrances and presenting endowments. Likewise, Master Hanuman, a monkey-confronted god, encapsulates characteristics of solidarity, commitment, and devotion.

Greek Folklore: Greek folklore incorporates divine beings and goddesses who take on creature frames or have creature credits. Dish, the lord of the wild, is frequently portrayed with the legs and horns of a goat, representing his association with nature. Artemis, the goddess of the chase, is regularly displayed with deer prongs on her head, meaning her job as a defender of natural life.

Local American Otherworldliness: Numerous Local American clans have their own tribal creatures and soul creatures with creature ascribes. These substances address the clan's personality and values. For example, the Navajo public worship the Corn Lady, a divinity with traits of the two people and plants. She means the fundamental association between farming, the development of corn, and the prosperity of the local area.

Antiquated Chinese Folklore: Chinese folklore incorporates various creature gods and spirits, each with explicit traits and jobs. The Sky blue Mythical beast, a venerated figure in Chinese culture, represents power and security. It is one of the four divine watchmen in Chinese folklore and is frequently portrayed with a mythical beast's body and a bird's nose.

The presence of zoomorphic gods in these customs mirrors the human interest with creatures and their representative importance. These heavenly creatures act as delegates, directing and safeguarding people and conveying moral and otherworldly examples.

Zoomorphism in Craftsmanship and Imagery

Zoomorphism is a typical theme in craftsmanship and imagery across various societies. It permits craftsmen and makers to consolidate human and creature components, leading to one of a kind and outwardly convincing portrayals. The utilization of zoomorphism in craftsmanship and imagery can convey different implications and subjects:

Creature Imagery: Zoomorphic craftsmanship frequently utilizes creature images to address characteristics or thoughts related with those creatures. For example, the owl, with its relationship with shrewdness and information, is a typical theme in libraries and instructive foundations, representing the quest for learning and illumination.

Social Personality: In many societies, zoomorphic images are utilized to address and build up social character. Chain of commands, for instance, are a conspicuous component of Native societies in North America. Every symbol creature on the post addresses a family's personality, values, and otherworldly association.

Legendary Accounts: Zoomorphic craftsmanship can portray scenes from fanciful accounts or stories that include divine beings or legends taking on creature shapes or connecting with creature creatures. These portrayals assist with conveying the fanciful and profound parts of the way of life.

Compositional Components: Zoomorphism frequently tracks down articulation in structural plans, where structures, sanctuaries, and landmarks consolidate creature themes. For instance, the sphinx, an animal with the body of a lion and the top of a human, has been a conspicuous design theme in Egypt and then some.

Brightening Expressions: Zoomorphic themes can be found in enhancing expressions like materials, ceramics, gems, and apparel. These plans frequently include creature examples and shapes, adding stylish allure and social importance to regular articles.

Zoomorphic workmanship and imagery improve the tasteful and social extravagance of different social orders, filling in for of articulation and conveying complex thoughts and convictions.

The Impact of Zoomorphism on Human Culture

Zoomorphism has affected human culture, influencing different parts of culture, otherworldliness, and human articulation:

Workmanship and Feel: Zoomorphism has been a significant wellspring of motivation for specialists from the beginning of time. It has affected the making of figures, works of art, enlivening expressions, and compositional plans, adding magnificence and social wealth to human development.

Social Character: Zoomorphic images assume a critical part in molding social personality. They frequently act as tokens of a local area's qualities, convictions, and shared legacy.

Religion and Otherworldliness: Zoomorphic divinities and spirits play played focal parts in strict and profound practices around the world. They act as mediators between the human and heavenly domains, offering direction and security.

Narrating and Folklore: The idea of zoomorphism is a common subject in folklore and narrating. It has given the establishment to innumerable fantasies, legends, and stories that convey moral and profound examples.

Ecological Mindfulness: The respect for creatures and the regular world, as typified in zoomorphic craftsmanship and imagery, has added to natural cognizance and stewardship. It underscores the interconnectedness among people and the climate.

5.3 Divine Shapeshifters and Hybrid Beings

Divine shapeshifters and half and half creatures are captivating and enchanted elements tracked down in different strict and legendary practices across the world. These elements have the remarkable capacity to change structure or show a mix of various structures, frequently mixing human and creature credits. The idea of shapeshifting and half breed creatures addresses a dynamic and complex part of human creative mind, offering experiences into our view of the real world and the otherworldly world. This exposition digs into the domain of heavenly shapeshifters and mixture creatures, investigating their beginnings, social importance, and representative implications in various social and strict settings.

Starting points of Heavenly Shapeshifters and Half breed Creatures

The idea of heavenly shapeshifters and half and half creatures has its beginnings in the aggregate human creative mind, with impacts from different sources:

Folklore and Fables: Legends and old stories from different societies frequently highlight creatures equipped for shapeshifting or existing in crossover structures. These accounts act as an impression of human interest with change and the craving to investigate the limits between various domains.

Animism and Nature Love: Numerous early social orders rehearsed animism, where regular components, creatures, and spirits were viewed as indispensable to day to day existence. This respect for the regular world impacted the idea of half and half creatures and shapeshifters, as creatures and normal peculiarities were frequently viewed as strong and enchanted.

Strict Convictions: In strict settings, divinities and spirits with the capacity to shapeshift or show up in cross breed structures assume a part in conveying the power and greatness of the heavenly. This idea mirrors that the heavenly is outside human ability to grasp and can take on different structures.

Supernatural quality and Otherworldliness: Shapeshifting and crossover creatures are often connected with magical and profound encounters. Shamans, for instance, frequently go through shapeshifting encounters during their daze like customs, where they speak with the soul world and take on various structures.

Social Meaning of Heavenly Shapeshifters and Crossover Creatures

Divine shapeshifters and crossover creatures convey significant social importance in the strict, imaginative, and legendary accounts of different societies. Their jobs and properties frequently reflect the qualities, convictions, and perspectives of the social orders that love them. The social meaning of these substances can be grasped in more than one way:

Crossing over Domains: Divine shapeshifters and mixture creatures frequently act as go-betweens between the human and profound domains. They address the interconnectedness of various aspects and work with correspondence between the two.

Imagery and Moral story: These elements often typify further emblematic implications. Their changes and half and half structures convey complex thoughts, frequently investigating subjects of duality, change, and the obscured limits between various conditions.

Profound Examples: Divine shapeshifters and half breed creatures highlight unmistakably in strict and legendary stories, conveying moral and otherworldly illustrations. They are utilized to show values, moral direct, and experiences into the human condition.

Social Character: These elements are symbolic of a culture's personality and perspective. They add uniqueness to the social account and become an essential piece of the shared awareness.

Creative Articulation: Divine shapeshifters and half breed creatures have motivated incalculable masterpieces. Craftsmen frequently investigate the stylish and representative parts of these substances through model, painting, and other creative structures.

Representative Implications of Shapeshifting and Half breed Structures

The capacity of heavenly shapeshifters and half and half creatures to change or show blended structures conveys rich emblematic implications:

Change and Variation: Shapeshifting exemplifies the idea of change and flexibility, representing the always changing nature of life and the significance of being adaptable and open to change.

Duality and Solidarity: Crossover creatures, with their mix of various structures, address the combination of alternate extremes. They typify the possibility that solidarity can be tracked down in variety, and that alternate extremes can coincide agreeably.

Otherworldly Edification: Shapeshifting can address profound development and illumination, meaning the excursion from one condition of being to a higher, more edified one.

Secret Insights: Shapeshifting frequently covers stowed away bits of insight or substitute real factors. These elements can uncover the inconspicuous or challenge our impression of the real world.

Social Varieties in Divine Shapeshifters and Half and half Creatures

Divine shapeshifters and half and half creatures take on different structures and jobs in various social settings. Each culture saturates these elements with its novel qualities, convictions, and emblematic implications. Here are a few models:

Greek Folklore: Greek folklore highlights Proteus, a heavenly shapeshifter and prophetic ocean god who can expect different structures, including creatures, components, and plants. Proteus encapsulates the possibility of change and flexibility, mirroring the consistently changing nature of the ocean.

Local American Otherworldliness: Numerous Local American clans have their own shapeshifting and mixture creatures, frequently connected with tribal creatures or watchman spirits. The Thunderbird, for instance, is a strong being fit for taking on various structures, addressing the powers of nature and the duality of creation and obliteration.

Hinduism: Hindu folklore incorporates gods and spirits with the capacity to accept different structures. Master Vishnu, a primary divinity in Hinduism, takes on various symbols to reestablish enormous equilibrium and keep up with dharma (honorableness). His symbols incorporate the human-like Rama, the pig headed Varaha, and the half-human, half-lion Narasimha.

Celtic Folklore: In Celtic folklore, the selkie is a shapeshifting being fit for changing from a seal into a human. The selkie addresses the duality of nature, typifying the possibility that the limits between the human and normal universes are liquid.

Japanese Legends: Kitsune are fox spirits in Japanese old stories known for their shapeshifting skills. Kitsune can change into human structure, frequently showing up as ladies. They represent both wickedness and generosity and are related with the Inari, the Shinto divinity of rice and success.

In every one of these social settings, divine shapeshifters and crossover creatures convey exceptional parts of their particular conviction frameworks and perspectives. They serve different jobs, including showing illustrations, intervening among universes, and investigating the secrets of presence.

Creative Articulations of Heavenly Shapeshifters and Half and half Creatures

The creative portrayals of heavenly shapeshifters and half and half creatures are a fundamental part of their social articulation. Craftsmen utilize different mediums, including model, painting, and ceremonies, to portray these substances and convey their imagery. Here are a few normal types of imaginative articulation:

Model and Sculptures: Many societies make complex figures and sculptures of heavenly shapeshifters and mixture creatures. These portrayals frequently catch the groundbreaking idea of these elements and their capacity to take on various structures.

Canvases and Iconography: The utilization of artworks and iconography permits specialists to portray these substances in different structures and settings. These pictures are much of the time utilized in strict customs, stories, and as helps in contemplation and supplication.

Customs and Functions: Divine shapeshifters and mixture creatures are much of the time summoned in strict customs and services. These customs act for the purpose of interfacing with the extraordinary and otherworldly parts of these elements.

Narrating and Folklore: Accounts and anecdotes about these elements are many times elapsed down through oral customs, composed texts, and legendary stories. These accounts assist with conveying the social importance and emblematic implications of heavenly shapeshifters and cross breed creatures to people in the future.

The Impact of Heavenly Shapeshifters and Crossover Creatures on Human Culture

Divine shapeshifters and half and half creatures have affected human culture in different ways, molding social, strict, and imaginative articulations. Their impact is obvious in:

Workmanship and Style: Divine shapeshifters and half and half creatures have roused specialists since the beginning of time, impacting the making of models, artworks, and other imaginative articulations. They add stylish lavishness and profundity to human imagination.

Social Character: These substances are meaningful of a culture's personality, forming its strict and legendary stories. They add to the uniqueness of a culture's perspective and personality.

Religion and Otherworldliness: Divine shapeshifters and crossover creatures frequently assume focal parts in strict customs and works on, filling in as go-betweens between the human and profound domains.

Narrating and Folklore: The idea of heavenly shapeshifters and crossover creatures is a common topic in folklore and narrating. It gives the establishment to incalculable fantasies, legends, and stories that convey moral and profound illustrations.

Social Solidarity: In many societies, the idea of heavenly shapeshifters and mixture creatures supports a feeling of social solidarity. They act as images of aggregate convictions and values.

Chapter 6

Animals in Rituals and Ceremonies

Creatures play had a focal impact in the customs and services of human social orders from the beginning of time. The connection among people and creatures is profoundly interlaced, enveloping different aspects, including social, strict, emblematic, and down to earth. Creatures have been worshiped, forfeited, and celebrated in functions and ceremonies, filling in as go-betweens between the human and otherworldly universes. This article investigates the diverse association among creatures and customs, analyzing their jobs in various social and strict settings, the imagery they convey, and the moral contemplations encompassing their utilization in services.

The Authentic and Social Meaning of Creatures in Customs

Creatures have been a piece of human customs and services for centuries, and their utilization has developed after some time. The authentic and social meaning of creatures in customs can be grasped from different perspectives:

Otherworldliness and Religion: Numerous old religions integrated creature penances for of speaking with the heavenly. In these unique circumstances, creatures were presented as gifts to divinities, and their penance was accepted to mollify or acquire favor from the divine beings. For instance, in old Greece, creature penances were a typical practice in the love of divine beings like Zeus and Apollo.

Imagery and Totemism: Creatures frequently hold representative implications in societies around the world. They might represent characteristics like strength, shrewdness, or fruitfulness. A few societies rehearsed totemism, where explicit creatures or creature spirits were viewed as progenitors or defenders of families and clans.

Agrarian and Occasional Ceremonies: Creatures have been necessary to rural and occasional customs that mark the patterns of planting, reaping, and richness. Such functions are frequently connected with the changing of seasons and the food of networks.

Mending and Divination: In numerous native social orders, creatures assume a part in recuperating and divination services. Shamans and medication men utilize creature imagery and creature parts in ceremonies intended to bring recuperating and knowledge.

Emblematic Reenactments: In certain societies, ceremonies include the representative reenactment of fantasies or accounts including creatures. These reenactments might be performed to recognize verifiable occasions or show significant moral examples.

Creatures in Strict Customs and Penances

Strict ceremonies and creature penances have been a basic piece of numerous old and contemporary conviction frameworks. The job of creatures in these practices fluctuates relying upon the particular strict custom and its related convictions. The following are a couple of models:

Antiquated Egyptian Religion: In old Egypt, creatures like cows, bulls, and ibises were frequently forfeited as contributions to the divine beings. The creatures were accepted to be middle people between the human and heavenly domains, conveying messages and petitions to the divine beings. They were likewise viewed as images of heavenly characteristics.

Hinduism: Hindu strict customs, particularly in sanctuary love, frequently include the utilization of creatures like cows, goats, and pigeons as conciliatory contributions. These ceremonies are accepted to sanitize the admirers and lay out an association with the heavenly. In a few Hindu factions, the idea of ahimsa (peacefulness) has prompted a decrease in creature penances.

Yoruba Religion: In Yoruba religion, rehearsed in West Africa and the African diaspora, creature penances are a focal part of associating with hereditary spirits and gods. Penances can incorporate chickens, goats, or bigger creatures like cows, contingent upon the meaning of the custom.

Judaism: In the Jewish custom, creature penances were once drilled as consumed contributions in the First and Second Sanctuaries in Jerusalem. These contributions were viewed as a method for looking for penance and speak with God. Notwithstanding, following the obliteration of the Subsequent Sanctuary, creature penances became out of date in Judaism.

Native and Shamanic Customs: Numerous native societies all over the planet have shamanic rehearses that include the utilization of creature parts in customs and mending functions. Creature bones, plumes, and stows away might be utilized in divination, recuperating, and otherworldly correspondence.

Moral Contemplations and Contentions

The utilization of creatures in strict ceremonies and penances has been a subject of moral discussion and contention. Key contemplations include:

Creature Government assistance: Pundits contend that creature penances in ceremonies can be unfeeling and make superfluous enduring creatures. Now and again, creatures might be abused or killed en masse, raising worries about remorselessness.

Social Awareness: Moving toward conversations of creature penances in strict settings with social sensitivity is fundamental. Various social orders have differing convictions and practices, and understanding the social importance is vital while tending to this point.

Options: A few strict customs and specialists have begun to investigate options in contrast to creature penances. For instance, plant-based contributions or emblematic motions might be utilized to address the soul of the penance without hurting creatures.

Legitimate Guidelines: A few nations have carried out guidelines with respect to the treatment of creatures in customs, guaranteeing their empathetic treatment and butcher. Offsetting strict opportunity with creature government assistance concerns stays a test.

Creatures in Emblematic and Memorial Customs

Creatures assume a critical part in emblematic and dedicatory customs that celebrate and respect social practices and verifiable occasions. These customs are much of the time set apart by energetic and happy functions. Here are a few models:

Chinese New Year: The Chinese New Year, otherwise called the Spring Celebration, is praised with different creature images addressing various years in the lunar schedule. Every year is related with a zodiac creature, and the celebrations incorporate motorcades, firecrackers, and the utilization of creature images to bring best of luck and success.

Mexican Day of the Dead: The Day of the Dead, or Dia de los Muertos, is a Mexican occasion that respects expired friends and family. Marigold blossoms and sugar skulls are frequently used to make special stepped areas, and beautiful papier-mâché or wooden creature figures, for example, calacas (skeletons), are shown to address the spirits of the departed.

Local American Powwows: Local American powwows are social affairs that celebrate and safeguard native practices. These occasions frequently incorporate moves, tunes, and elaborate ensembles, for example, customary creature crowns and formal attire, which hold profound representative importance.

Jewish Passover: The Passover Seder, a fundamental piece of the Jewish Passover occasion, incorporates the emblematic utilization of a leg of lamb bone and a hard-bubbled egg, which address parts of the Departure story and the recharging of life.

African and Caribbean Amusement parks: Fairs in Africa and the Caribbean highlight energetic motorcades, music, and moves. Members frequently wear elaborate outfits that might incorporate creature themes, like padded covers, emblems, and creature roused body paint.

Creatures as Emblems and Images in Native Societies

Native societies overall have a profound and otherworldly association with creatures, which frequently act as emblems and images of social character. Emblems are creatures or other regular components that are accepted to have a unique relationship with a faction, clan, or local area. They can address familial spirits, defenders, and wellsprings of direction. The utilization of creature emblems is a strong method for communicating social character and otherworldly association. The following are a couple of models:

Local American Symbols: Local American clans have creature emblems that address their family or clan's personality and values. Emblem creatures can incorporate the hawk, wolf, bear, and turtle, each representing various characteristics and lessons.

Australian Native Dreamtime: In Australian Native societies, dreamtime stories and emblems highlight creatures like the kangaroo, emu, and crocodile. These symbols are basic to the social and otherworldly personality of various Native gatherings.

African Tribal Spirits: In numerous African social orders, creatures are viewed as progenitors or spirits that give direction and security. Symbols like the lion, panther, and elephant are huge in these societies.

Inuit Creature Spirits: In Inuit culture, creatures like the polar bear, walrus, and caribou are seen as creature spirits and wellsprings of direction. The Inuit have unpredictable stories and customs related with these spirits.

Celtic Creature Images: In Celtic customs, creatures like the stag, raven, and salmon are related with explicit characteristics and lessons. These creatures frequently show up in Celtic craftsmanship and imagery, mirroring the social personality of the Celts.

The utilization of creature emblems and images in native societies builds up the association among people and the regular world, advancing a feeling of solidarity and congruity with the climate.

Creatures in Present day Services and Celebrations

While a few customary practices keep on remembering creatures for their ceremonies and services, others have developed to adjust to changing social standards and moral contemplations. In current functions and celebrations, creatures might be engaged with a more sympathetic and emblematic way. The following are a couple of models:

Bullfighting: Bullfighting, which has confronted huge analysis for creature remorselessness, has developed to incorporate more accommodating varieties, like Portuguese-style bullfighting, where the bull isn't killed in the field. A few present day bullfights utilize representative strips as opposed to harming the bull.

Running of the Bulls: The Running of the Bulls in Pamplona, Spain, has developed to diminish mischief to the creatures. At times, the bulls are not generally killed in the bullring, and wellbeing measures for both the creatures and members have been moved along.

Creature Favors: In certain societies and strict practices, creatures are honored as a feature of functions and celebrations, for example, the yearly gift of pets at Catholic temples. These favors advance the government assistance of creatures and commend the human-creature bond.

Basic entitlements Activism: Basic entitlements activists have effectively campaigned for changes in services and celebrations including creatures, prompting expanded mindfulness and assurance for creatures. A few customs have adjusted to limit mischief to creatures or have ended specific practices.

Compassionate Meat and Food Celebrations: A few celebrations that generally highlighted creature penances or the hunting of creatures have changed to zero in on the others conscious readiness and utilization of meat. This approach underlines the significance of moral obtaining and feasible practices.

While a few conventional works on including creatures stay, the world is seeing a shift towards more empathetic and moral treatment of creatures in functions and celebrations, reflecting changing cultural qualities and a developing familiarity with creature government assistance.

6.1 Sacrificial Animals and Ritualistic Practices

Conciliatory creatures and the related ceremonial practices have been a necessary piece of human culture and religion for centuries. The demonstration of offering creatures as penances in strict and social functions is a complex and well established custom that changes across various societies and conviction frameworks. This article investigates the verifiable and social meaning of conciliatory creatures, the different customs related with their utilization, the moral contemplations encompassing these practices, and the advancement of conciliatory practices in present day times.

The Verifiable and Social Meaning of Conciliatory Creatures

Conciliatory works on including creatures have a long and different history that can be followed back to old civilizations. The meaning of these practices is profoundly implanted in the social and strict accounts of different social orders. The verifiable and social significance of conciliatory creatures can be grasped through a few key aspects:

Strict Convictions: Conciliatory creatures assume a focal part in numerous strict practices. These customs are frequently viewed as demonstrations of dedication, dutifulness, and accommodation to divine substances. By offering creatures to divine beings or gods, experts look to lay out an association with the otherworldly domain.

Imagery and Amends: Creatures in conciliatory ceremonies frequently address representative implications and should be visible as substitutes or images of expiation. The demonstration of offering a creature as a penance is accepted to scrub or filter the admirer from sins or offenses.

Farming Importance: In horticultural social orders, ceremonies including conciliatory animals are frequently attached to the patterns of planting, gathering, and richness. These services look to guarantee a plentiful gather and the prosperity of the local area.

Common Solidarity: Conciliatory functions are many times public occasions that encourage a feeling of solidarity and shared character inside a local area or strict gathering. They can build up friendly bonds and social customs.

Moral and Moral Examples: A few conciliatory practices are expected to convey moral and moral illustrations. For instance, they might accentuate the significance of altruism, lowliness, or dedication.

Conciliatory Creatures in Various Societies and Religions

The utilization of conciliatory creatures is inescapable and changes essentially across various societies and strict practices. Every custom has its own convictions, rehearses, and representative implications related with conciliatory creatures. The following are a couple of models from different social and strict settings:

Hinduism: Creature penances, especially of cows and goats, have been a well established practice in certain organizations of Hinduism. Penances are many times acted in sanctuaries and strict services as contributions to divinities. The conciliatory meat is then conveyed to the local area as prasadam (blessed food).

Old Greece: Creature penances, especially of bulls, were a typical component in old Greek strict customs. These ceremonies were led to assuage different divine beings and goddesses and to look for favor or direction.

Judaism: In antiquated Judaism, creature penances were vital to adore in the First and Second Sanctuaries in Jerusalem. These penances were viewed as demonstrations of dutifulness to God and were performed to make amends for sins. Notwithstanding, following the obliteration of the Subsequent Sanctuary, creature penances became outdated in Judaism.

Santeria: Santeria is a syncretic religion that started in Cuba and mixes components of Yoruba religion with Catholicism. Creature penances are an indispensable piece of Santeria ceremonies, where explicit creatures like chickens and goats are proposed to respect and speak with orishas (gods).

Vedic Customs: In Vedic practices of India, conciliatory ceremonies known as yajnas include the contribution of different substances, including ghee, grains, and sometimes creatures, into a sacrosanct fire. The conviction is that these contributions sanitize and conciliate the divinities.

Native Societies: Numerous native societies practice creature penances in customs and services. These practices shift generally, with some including the penance of creatures like chickens, goats, or bison to respect familial spirits and divinities.

Moral Contemplations and Contentions

The utilization of creatures in conciliatory ceremonies has raised critical moral worries and debates. Key contemplations include:

Creature Government assistance: Pundits contend that creature penances in customs can be obtuse and make superfluous enduring creatures. At times, creatures might be abused or killed en masse, raising worries about savagery.

Social Awareness: Moving toward conversations of creature penances in strict settings with social sensitivity is fundamental. Various social orders have differing convictions and practices, and understanding the social importance is vital while tending to this point.

Choices: A few strict customs and experts have begun to investigate options in contrast to creature penances. For instance, plant-based contributions or emblematic signals might be utilized to address the soul of the penance without hurting creatures.

Legitimate Guidelines: A few nations have carried out guidelines with respect to the treatment of creatures in ceremonies, guaranteeing their empathetic treatment and butcher. Offsetting strict opportunity with creature government assistance concerns stays a test.

Ceremonial Practices and Imagery

Conciliatory works on including creatures frequently consolidate elaborate ceremonies with representative components. These ceremonies might incorporate explicit signals, supplications, contributions, and emblematic demonstrations that upgrade the otherworldly or representative significance of the penance. Ceremonial practices are fundamental for the conciliatory interaction and fill a few needs:

Association with the Heavenly: Ceremonies make a consecrated space and air for speaking with the heavenly. They frequently include petitions, mantras, or summons to conjure the presence of divine beings or divinities.

Purging and Expiation: Ceremonies in conciliatory practices frequently refine the admirer and offer penance for sins or offenses. These demonstrations of cleansing might incorporate the sprinkling of sacred water or the recitation of explicit supplications.

Representative Components: Ceremonies might consolidate emblematic components, like the utilization of explicit tones, apparel, or contributions. These images might address virtue, modesty, or commitment.

Local area Contribution: Numerous conciliatory ceremonies are common occasions, and customs effectively join the local area in love. These aggregate demonstrations of commitment fortify social bonds and shared personality.

Authentic and Fanciful Stories: A few ceremonies are intended to reenact or honor verifiable occasions or legendary accounts. This helps protect social and strict customs and lessons.

Development of Conciliatory Practices in Present day Times

Conciliatory practices including creatures have developed and adjusted to present day times because of moral worries, lawful guidelines, and changing cultural qualities. A few patterns mirror this development:

Decrease in Creature Forfeits: A few strict customs have diminished the recurrence and size of creature penances in light of moral worries. Now and again, creature penances have been supplanted with emblematic signals, like contribution blossoms or natural products.

Accentuation on Moral Butcher: In locales where creature penances proceed, there is much of the time a developing accentuation on moral treatment and empathetic butcher of creatures. Guidelines have been set up to guarantee the government assistance of conciliatory creatures.

Plant-Based Other options: In a few strict practices, plant-based contributions are being utilized as options in contrast to creature penances. This lines up with a developing worldwide pattern toward vegetarianism and veganism.

Lawful Guidelines: Numerous nations have executed legitimate guidelines to oversee the treatment of creatures in strict ceremonies. These guidelines expect to offset strict opportunity with creature government assistance.

Interfaith Exchanges: Interfaith discoursed and conversations on the moral treatment of creatures in strict practices are encouraging a superior comprehension of contrasting viewpoints. This discourse can prompt more comprehensive and caring methodologies.

6.2 Animal Festivals and Celebrations

Creature celebrations and festivities are assorted and dynamic occasions that occur all over the planet, exhibiting the profound social associations among people and creatures. These celebrations include different perspectives, like regarding creatures, bringing issues to light about their protection, and advancing social legacy. The social meaning of these celebrations is multi-faceted, including customs, otherworldliness, and ecological mindfulness. This paper investigates the variety of creature celebrations and festivities, their social significance, and their effect on both nearby and worldwide networks.

The Social Meaning of Creature Celebrations

Creature celebrations and festivities are established in the social customs and conviction frameworks of the social orders that training them. These celebrations hold social importance in more ways than one:

Conventional and Verifiable Roots: Numerous creature celebrations have been commended for quite a long time, mirroring the verifiable and customary traditions of a local area or district. These practices are gone down through ages, building up social character.

Social Legacy: Creature celebrations frequently act for of saving social legacy. They give a stage to the transmission of information, values, and customs to more youthful ages, guaranteeing the progression of social practices.

Local area Union: These festivals encourage a feeling of local area and solidarity. They unite individuals in shared exercises, fortifying social bonds and aggregate character.

Otherworldly and Strict Associations: In certain societies, creature celebrations have profound or strict importance. They act as a method for communicating commitment to gods or to respect creatures considered sacrosanct.

Ecological Mindfulness: Numerous creature celebrations underscore the significance of untamed life preservation and the assurance of regular natural surroundings. These festivals frequently incorporate instructive parts that bring issues to light about the climate and the requirement for dependable stewardship.

Various Creature Celebrations and Festivities

Creature celebrations and festivities come in different structures and are commended all over the planet. They feature the wealth and variety of social articulations connected with creatures. The following are a couple of models:

Diwali (India): Diwali, otherwise called the Celebration of Lights, is perhaps of the main celebration in Hinduism. During Diwali, creatures, for example, cows and elephants are embellished with beautifying adornments and marched through the roads. This training represents the heavenly idea of creatures and the human-creature bond.

Elephant Celebrations (Different Areas): Elephant celebrations are praised in nations like Thailand and Nepal, where elephants are profoundly adored. These celebrations incorporate processions, conventional services, and elephant-focused exercises. They feature the social meaning of elephants and advance their preservation.

La Tomatina (Spain): La Tomatina is a yearly celebration held in the Spanish town of Buñol. While not solely centered around creatures, the celebration incorporates the running of bulls through the roads, a practice that has confronted analysis for its treatment of creatures. As of late, the celebration has moved toward additional empathetic practices.

Dia de los Muertos (Mexico): Dia de los Muertos, or the Day of the Dead, is a Mexican occasion that respects perished friends and family. Creature figures, for example, sugar skulls and marigold blossoms, are utilized to adorn raised areas and praise the spirits of the withdrew. These images mirror the profound association among creatures and the otherworldly world.

Songkran (Thailand): Songkran is the Thai New Year festivity, set apart by water battles and different exercises. In certain districts of Thailand, the celebration incorporates the arrival of creatures, for example, fish and birds as a type of legitimacy making, established in Buddhist convictions.

Yanshui Bee colony Firecrackers Celebration (Taiwan): The Yanshui Colony of bees Firecrackers Celebration in Taiwan includes a novel and thinking for even a second to practice of sending off firecrackers. Members use fireworks and rockets to make a stunning presentation while wearing defensive stuff to protect themselves from the unstable sparkles. The celebration has authentic and otherworldly roots and is related with heading out abhorrent spirits.

Running of the Bulls (Spain): The Running of the Bulls in Pamplona, Spain, is an undeniably popular occasion where individuals run close by a gathering of bulls through the roads. While this celebration has been condemned for creature savagery, lately, security measures have been improved to safeguard both the creatures and members.

Social Articulations and Imaginative Manifestations

Creature celebrations frequently motivate imaginative articulations that mirror the social meaning of these festivals. Different types of workmanship, including music, dance, visual expressions, and specialties, are made to catch the quintessence of these celebrations. These imaginative manifestations assume a fundamental part in safeguarding the social legacy related with creature festivities.

Music and Dance: Numerous creature celebrations include customary music and dance exhibitions that feature the social personality of the local area. These articulations might include special instruments, rhythms, and dance styles related with the celebration.

Visual Expressions: Craftsmen frequently make works of art, models, and other visual fine arts that portray the creatures celebrated in these celebrations. These fine arts act as both social antiques and articulations of respect for the creatures.

Ornamental Expressions: Celebrations like Diwali and Dia de los Muertos include the formation of mind boggling improvements, including vivid rangoli plans and elaborate sugar skulls. These ornamental expressions are a crucial piece of the celebration customs.

Specialties and Outfits: Numerous creature celebrations highlight the production of artworks and ensembles that mirror the celebration's topic. These things are frequently hand tailored, utilizing conventional strategies and materials.

Verse and Writing: Sonnets, stories, and scholarly works frequently catch the quintessence of creature celebrations, giving a story that extends the comprehension of the social and representative implications related with these festivals.

Natural Mindfulness and Preservation

A few creature celebrations consolidate natural mindfulness and preservation endeavors as a feature of their festivals. These celebrations advance mindful stewardship of the climate and natural life protection. They act as stages for teaching participants and bringing issues to light about biological issues.

The following are a couple of manners by which creature celebrations add to natural mindfulness and preservation:

Instructive Projects: Numerous creature celebrations incorporate instructive parts, like talks, studios, and displays about natural life preservation and ecological issues. These projects illuminate people in general about the significance regarding safeguarding normal natural surroundings and imperiled species.

Gathering pledges for Preservation: A few creature celebrations utilize their occasions as any open doors to raise assets for protection associations and drives. These assets might uphold untamed life insurance and natural surroundings reclamation endeavors.

Untamed life Asylums and Recovery: In a few creature celebrations, participants get the opportunity to find out about and visit untamed life safe-havens and restoration focuses. These offices center around the salvage and restoration of creatures, bringing issues to light about the difficulties they face.

Maintainable Practices: Creature celebrations might embrace feasible and eco-accommodating practices, like diminishing plastic waste, advancing mindful the travel industry, and limiting their biological impression.

Local area Contribution: Creature celebrations frequently empower the support of neighborhood networks in ecological drives and protection endeavors, cultivating a feeling of obligation and stewardship.

The Effect of Creature Celebrations on Networks

Creature celebrations significantly affect the networks that celebrate them. They act as central focuses for social attachment, social personality, and monetary development. The effect of these celebrations on networks incorporates:

Financial Lift: Creature celebrations can monetarily affect the host networks. They draw in sightseers and guests, prompting expanded income for neighborhood organizations, including lodgings, cafés, and craftsman markets.

Social Safeguarding: These celebrations assume a fundamental part in protecting social legacy. They give a stage to the transmission of conventional information, values, and customs to more youthful ages, guaranteeing the congruity of social practices.

Social Union: Creature celebrations encourage a feeling of local area and solidarity. They unite individuals in shared exercises, reinforcing social bonds and aggregate personality.

Social Trade: Numerous creature celebrations draw in worldwide guests, advancing social trade and understanding. They set out open doors for intercultural discoursed and the sharing of customs.

Mindfulness and Preservation: Creature celebrations add to ecological mindfulness and protection endeavors, empowering neighborhood networks to play a functioning job in safeguarding their regular habitat.

Moral Contemplations and Difficulties

Regardless of their social importance and positive effect on networks, a few creature celebrations face moral difficulties and debates. These worries ordinarily rotate around the treatment of creatures associated with these festivals. Key moral contemplations include:

Creature Government assistance: A few creature celebrations have been censured for their treatment of creatures. Rehearses that include damage, mercilessness, or the double-dealing of creatures have confronted reaction from creature government assistance advocates.

Preservation Issues: The catch or utilization of wild creatures in celebrations might add to protection challenges, as it can adversely affect untamed life populaces. A few celebrations have pushed toward additional economical practices or elective festivals that don't hurt creatures.

Wellbeing Concerns: Certain creature celebrations can present dangers to the two members and creatures. The running of the bulls in Pamplona, for instance, has been related with wounds to the two people and creatures.

Social Awareness: Conversations encompassing the morals of creature celebrations should be drawn nearer with social responsiveness, taking into account the assorted convictions and customs of various social orders.

The Eventual fate of Creature Celebrations

As the world turns out to be more interconnected and earth cognizant, the eventual fate of creature celebrations is probably going to go through changes. A few patterns and conceivable outcomes include:

Accentuation on Moral Treatment: Numerous creature celebrations are progressing toward more sympathetic and moral treatment of creatures, diminishing damage and mercilessness.

Natural Manageability: Celebrations might put a more grounded accentuation on ecological maintainability, taking on eco-accommodating practices and advancing untamed life protection.

Schooling and Mindfulness: The instructive parts of creature celebrations will probably keep on developing, bringing issues to light about untamed life and environmental issues.

Social Trade: Creature celebrations will keep on drawing in global guests, cultivating social trade and understanding.

Elective Festivals: at times, creature celebrations might develop into elective festivals that don't include damage to creatures.

6.3 The Role of Animals in Divination

Since forever ago, the regular world and its animals play had a critical impact in human social orders, frequently filling in as wellsprings of motivation and direction. In divination, the act of looking for information or understanding through extraordinary means, creatures have been significant specialists and images. Different societies across the world have integrated creatures into divinatory works on, ascribing them with otherworldly and emblematic importance. This exposition investigates the job of creatures in divination, the variety of divinatory strategies, and the emblematic implications and social translations related with these practices.

The Variety of Divinatory Techniques Including Creatures

Divination is a diverse practice, and it consolidates many techniques and devices for looking for knowledge and direction. While creatures assume a focal part in numerous divinatory practices, they are utilized in different ways. Here are a portion of the different divinatory techniques including creatures:

Divination: Prognostication is a training that includes deciphering the way of behaving and flight examples of birds, like falcons or crows, to acquire bits of knowledge into what's in store. In old Rome, forecasts noticed the trip of birds to make expectations and deal direction.

Zoomancy: Zoomancy, otherwise called theriomancy, is the act of divination through the perception of the way of behaving, developments, or attributes of creatures. This strategy is boundless and frequently includes the translation of creature signs and signs.

Ichthyomancy: Ichthyomancy is a type of divination that utilizations fish as the essential instrument. The development and conduct of fish in an assigned waterway are noticed and deciphered to uncover future occasions or answer explicit inquiries.

Creature Cards: A few divinatory frameworks use decks of cards or prophet cards highlighting creature pictures. These cards are attracted or rearranged to give bits of knowledge, similar as tarot cards or runes.

Ovomancy: Ovomancy, otherwise called oomancy, includes divination through the understanding of eggs. It can incorporate techniques like perusing the examples shaped by egg whites when broken, or noticing the development of yolks inside an egg.

Entrail Divination: In certain societies, creature guts, especially the liver, were utilized for divination. The antiquated Etruscans, for instance, rehearsed haruspicy, which included inspecting the insides of forfeited creatures to make expectations.

Symbol Creatures: Local American clans and different native societies all over the planet have embraced the idea of emblem creatures. Emblem creatures act as other-worldly aides and wellsprings of insight, and their imagery is integrated into divinatory practices.

The Emblematic Implications and Social Translations of Creature Divination

The utilization of creatures in divination goes past the simple perception of their way of behaving; it is well established in imagery and social understandings. The emblematic implications of creatures fluctuate across various societies and conviction frameworks. Here are a few instances of creature imagery in divination:

Birds: Birds are frequently connected with opportunity, profound messages, and correspondence with the heavenly. The particular sorts of birds and their conduct convey remarkable emblematic implications. For instance, the owl is viewed as an image of insight, while the raven can address change or change.

Bugs: Bugs like butterflies, honey bees, and subterranean insects are viewed as images of change, local area, and steadiness, individually. The way of behaving and presence of these bugs can be deciphered to give direction or experiences.

Reptiles and Creatures of land and water: Reptiles and creatures of land and water, like snakes and frogs, are frequently connected with change and resurrection. The shedding of a snake's skin or the transformation of a frog are viewed as representative of individual change.

Warm blooded animals: Various vertebrates have unmistakable emblematic implications. For example, the bear might address contemplation and reflective idea, while the wolf is frequently connected with senses and instinct.

Fish: Fish are images of overflow, richness, and flexibility. The heading and developments of fish in water can be deciphered to offer experiences around one's conditions.

Homegrown Creatures: Homegrown creatures like felines, canines, and ponies have interesting imagery in view of their connections with people. Canines, for instance, are frequently connected with dependability and security, while felines might represent freedom and instinct.

Social understandings of creature divination additionally draw from neighborhood fables, folklore, and verifiable setting. In certain societies, creatures act as couriers or middle people between the human and otherworldly domains. The particular implications credited to creatures can be profoundly imbued in the shared perspective of a general public, it are led to shape the way divinatory practices.

Creature Divination and Human-Creature Association

The utilization of creatures in divination mirrors the getting through human-creature association, which has been a basic piece of human culture and otherworldliness since the beginning of time. This association reaches out past the emblematic domain and holds a few ramifications:

Go-betweens: Creatures are frequently viewed as mediators among people and the profound world. They are accepted to have remarkable experiences and admittance to stowed away information, making them important in divinatory practices.

Solidarity with Nature: Divinatory works on including creatures advance a feeling of solidarity with the regular world. They stress the interconnectedness of every single living being and support an all encompassing viewpoint on life.

Direction and Backing: Numerous divinatory frameworks including creatures offer direction, insight, and backing. The presence of a creature in a divinatory perusing can be deciphered as an indication of help or a significant message.

Individual Change: Creature imagery frequently addresses self-improvement and change. The experiences acquired from creature divination might urge people to think about their own life process and embrace change.

Social Character: The utilization of creatures in divination is a statement of social personality and legacy. It supports the novel convictions and upsides of various social orders and can act as a social standard.

Current Variations and Translations

While conventional divination strategies including creatures keep on being drilled in different societies, present day transformations have additionally arisen. These transformations might consolidate new advancements, for example, online creature themed divination applications or decks of cards including contemporary creature imagery. Certain individuals take part in creature divination as a type of thoughtfulness, individual reflection, or self improvement, as opposed to for explicit expectations or direction.

Also, the imagery of creatures in divination has been embraced by specific developments, like creature totemism in New Age otherworldliness. Emblem creatures are frequently utilized as images of individual qualities, direction, and life way, uplifting people to investigate their association with the collective of animals.

Moral Contemplations and Reactions

The act of creature divination has not been without its faultfinders and moral worries. A portion of the main points of interest raised include:

Creature Government assistance: Pundits contend that specific types of creature divination, especially those that include the penance or mischief of creatures, bring up moral issues about creature government assistance. Rehearses like haruspicy and different types of entrail divination have confronted specific examination.

Strange notion: Doubters battle that divination works on, including those including creatures, are established in notion and need logical legitimacy. They contend that such practices can propagate nonsensical convictions and mystical reasoning.

Social Allocation: A few pundits raise worries about social allotment when people from outside a specific culture embrace or adjust the divinatory acts of that culture. Appointment should be visible as insolent and harsh.

Protection: The utilization of specific creatures in divination might have preservation suggestions, as it might add to the interest for explicit species, influencing their populaces and regular environments.

Adjusting Social Customs and Moral Contemplations

Adjusting social customs and moral contemplations in the domain of creature divination is a perplexing undertaking. Social awareness and regard for assorted conviction frameworks are fundamental. Far to address moral worries include:

Advancement of Moral Practices: Backers for creature divination can advance practices that focus on creature government assistance and the compassionate treatment of creatures. Now and again, elective strategies or imagery might be thought of.

Discourse and Training: Participating in open exchange and teaching specialists and the general population about the moral ramifications of specific divination practices can encourage mindfulness and understanding.

Dependable The travel industry: In districts where creature based divination is worked on, advancing mindful the travel industry and moral creature experiences can assist with alleviating mischief to creatures.

Legitimate Guidelines: A few nations have executed lawful guidelines to oversee the treatment of creatures in divinatory practices. These guidelines plan to shield creatures from savagery and damage while regarding social practices.

Chapter 7

Folklore and Fables: Animal Stories and Morality Tales

Legends and tales are a fundamental piece of human narrating customs, mirroring the aggregate insight and upsides of various societies. Among the most persevering and all around valued types of fables are creature stories and profound quality stories. These accounts, highlighting creatures as focal characters, convey ageless examples and virtues while giving experiences into the human condition. This paper investigates the rich practice of creature stories and ethical quality stories in fables, their social importance, and the persevering through allure of these accounts across various social orders and time spans.

The Underlying foundations of Creature Stories in Fables

Creature stories have antiquated beginnings, tracing all the way back to the oral customs of many societies. The utilization of creatures as characters in these stories was a pragmatic and inventive decision. Creatures were recognizable to individuals and frequently displayed human-like ways of behaving and characteristics, making them interesting and reasonable for conveying moral examples. These accounts assisted with making sense of regular peculiarities, human ways of behaving, and the secrets of the world while giving diversion and guidance. The underlying foundations of creature stories in legends can be followed to different districts and societies, including:

Aesop's Tales (Old Greece): Aesop's Tales, ascribed to the old Greek narrator Aesop, are among the most popular assortments of creature stories. These short accounts use creatures as characters to delineate moral examples and are known for their persevering through pertinence.

Panchatantra (India): The Panchatantra, an old Sanskrit assortment of creature tales, is one of the most seasoned known works of Indian writing. These accounts, highlighting talking creatures, investigate topics of insight, crafty, and ethical quality.

Kalila and Dimna (Persia): Kalila and Dimna is a Persian assortment of creature tales that has been converted into numerous dialects and impacted narrating customs across the world. The stories spin around the fellowship between two jackals and bestow moral and moral examples.

African Fables: African legends is wealthy in creature stories, where creatures like Anansi the bug, Bunny, and Lion assume focal parts. These accounts are gone down through oral custom and are utilized to convey moral illustrations, social insight, and verifiable information.

Local American Practices: Different Local American clans have their own creature stories and fables. These stories frequently include creatures as focal figures and act for of sending social qualities and lessons.

The Social Meaning of Creature Stories and Profound quality Stories

Creature stories and profound quality stories play had a huge impact in forming societies and social orders, with a few layers of social importance:

Moral Guidance: These accounts are frequently used to convey moral and moral illustrations. They give direction on highminded conduct, moral navigation, and the outcomes of one's activities. The effortlessness of creature characters makes the ethical illustrations available to all progress in years gatherings.

Social Personality: Creature stories are profoundly implanted in the social character of various social orders. They mirror the qualities, convictions, and perspectives of a culture and act for the purpose of communicating that social legacy to people in the future.

Instructive Device: Creature stories are instructive apparatuses for showing values, normal practices, and fundamental abilities. They empower decisive reasoning, critical thinking, and sympathy, assisting people with pursuing moral decisions in their lives.

Amusement and Commitment: These accounts are engaging and connecting with, making them open to the two youngsters and grown-ups. They use humor, incongruity, and moral story to charm the crowd while granting significant examples.

Social Discourse: Creature stories can act as a type of social editorial, evaluating the human condition and cultural issues from the perspective of creature characters. They frequently uncover general bits of insight about human instinct and conduct.

People Insight: These accounts are a storehouse of society intelligence, epitomizing the aggregate encounters and information on a general public. They give knowledge into the difficulties and issues looked by changed societies from the beginning of time.

The General Allure of Creature Stories

Creature stories have a general allure that rises above social limits, and their getting through notoriety can be credited to a few elements:

Appeal: Creatures are natural and interesting to individuals of any age and foundations. They display a great many ways of behaving, qualities, and feelings that are like human encounters, making them simple to interface with.

Immortality: The ethical examples and topics in creature stories are ageless and resound across ages. They address crucial human qualities and problems that stay pertinent since forever ago.

Openness: Creature stories are much of the time basic and clear, making them available to a wide crowd, incorporating youngsters and those with changing degrees of proficiency.

Multifaceted Accounts: These accounts frequently contain various layers of importance and can be delighted in on various levels. Kids might see the value in the superficial story, while grown-ups can dig into more profound translations.

General Subjects: Creature stories investigate widespread topics like trustworthiness, benevolence, shrewdness, and the results of one's activities. These subjects are pertinent to individuals from different social foundations.

Key Topics in Creature Stories and Ethical quality Stories

Creature stories and profound quality stories frequently investigate various topics that give important life illustrations. A portion of the key subjects include:

The Significance of Shrewdness: Numerous creature stories stress the worth of insight and knowledge. Characters like the fox and the owl are much of the time depicted as insightful and tricky, while the silliness of different creatures fills in as a wake up call.

Genuineness and Honesty: Trustworthiness is a common topic in these accounts. Characters that untruth or delude others frequently face adverse results, featuring the significance of trustworthiness and honesty.

Graciousness and Sympathy: Benevolence and empathy are praised in numerous creature stories. Characters that offer grace to other people, in any event, when it isn't responded, are frequently depicted emphatically.

The Outcomes of Avarice: Covetousness and narrow-mindedness are normal subjects in creature stories. Characters that focus on their own advantages over others frequently endure negative fallouts.

Tirelessness and Assurance: Accounts of creatures conquering difficulties through persistence and assurance rouse perusers to never surrender, even notwithstanding misfortune.

Fellowship and Participation: Numerous creature stories accentuate the worth of companionship and collaboration. Characters that cooperate to accomplish a shared objective are frequently compensated.

The Risks of Haughtiness: Presumption and pride are much of the time portrayed as regrettable characteristics in these accounts. Characters that underrate others or brag about their capacities are as often as possible lowered.

Conspicuous Creature Characters in Fables

Various creature characters have become notable in the realm of old stories and tales. These characters, each with their remarkable qualities and illustrations, lastingly affect narrating customs. Probably the most unmistakable creature characters include:

The Turtle and the Rabbit: This exemplary tale, frequently ascribed to Aesop, shows the illustration that "unwavering mindsets always win in the end." The turtle's assurance and determination lead to triumph over the haughty and expedient bunny.

The Fox and the Grapes: One more tale from Aesop, this story includes a fox that can't arrive at a lot of grapes and excuses them as harsh. It fills in as an example in harsh grapes, defense, and the risks of self-duplicity.

The Lion and the Mouse: Aesop's tale about an empathetic mouse that helps a lion in trouble shows that even the powerless can be of extraordinary help to serious areas of strength for the. It passes on the message that thoughtfulness can be compensated.

The Three Little Pigs: This notable fantasy recounts the tale of three pigs who fabricate places of various materials (straw, sticks, and blocks) to safeguard themselves from a guile wolf. It shows the significance of difficult work and arranging.

The Kid Who Deceived everyone: This useful example underscores the results of misleading problems. It recounts the tale of a kid who more than once tells a shameful lie to stand out however isn't accepted when a genuine wolf shows up.

The Odd one out: Hans Christian Andersen's popular story investigates topics of character and self-acknowledgment. The odd one out, derided for its appearance, at last changes into a wonderful swan.

Anansi the Bug (African Legends): Anansi, a shrewd and crafty bug, is a famous person in African old stories. His accounts frequently rotate around his endeavors to outsmart others and get information, accentuating the significance of mind and keenness.

The Advancement of Creature Stories in Current Writing and Media

Creature stories and ethical quality stories lastingly affect writing and media. They keep on being adjusted and reconsidered in present day settings, taking care of contemporary crowds while safeguarding their moral and moral messages. A few prominent instances of the development of creature stories in present day writing and media include:

"Animal Homestead" by George Orwell: George Orwell's "Animal Ranch" is a sarcastic moral story that utilizes a gathering of livestock to study the defiling impact of force and the risks of tyranny. The story shows how even all that expectations can be ruined by eagerness and aspiration.

"Watership Down" by Richard Adams: "Watership Down" is an experience novel highlighting a gathering of hares looking for another home. The story dives into subjects of authority, dauntlessness, and local area. The characters' process reflects the battles and difficulties looked by human social orders.

Disney's Energized Movies: Disney has adjusted numerous exemplary creature stories, for example, "The Lion Lord" (enlivened by Shakespeare's "Hamlet") and "The Wilderness Book" (motivated by Rudyard Kipling's work). These transformations frequently investigate topics of family, obligation, and personality.

"Charlotte's Internet" by E.B. White: "Charlotte's Internet" is a cherished kids' clever that recounts the tale of a pig named Wilbur and his kinship with a shrewd insect named Charlotte. The novel investigates topics of companionship, penance, and the pattern of life.

Aesop's Tales in Kids' Writing: Aesop's Tales have been adjusted into various youngsters' books that acquaint youthful perusers with ageless moral examples through creature characters and basic accounts.

Enlivened Movies and TV: Vivified movies and TV series like "Zootopia," "Kung Fu Panda," and "The Lion Watchman" keep on utilizing creature characters to convey moral and moral examples in a connecting with and engaging way.

The Persevering through Tradition of Creature Stories and Ethical quality Stories

Creature stories and profound quality stories have left a getting through heritage in the realm of narrating and proceed to charm and teach crowds, everything being equal. The persevering through allure of these accounts can be credited to their capacity to pass complex moral and moral examples on through appealing and charming creature characters. These accounts rise above social limits and time spans, offering significant experiences into the human condition and the immortal quest for intelligence and excellence.

However long individuals look for direction, diversion, and moral guidance, creature stories and ethical quality stories will keep on holding an extraordinary spot in the domain of fables and writing. Their accounts of crafty foxes, insightful owls, and valiant bunnies will stay loved and passed down starting with one age then onto the next, guaranteeing that the illustrations they give stay as applicable and important as anyone might think possible.

7.1 Aesop's Fables and Animal Morality

Aesop's Tales, an assortment of old Greek stories credited to the narrator Aesop, are among the most persevering and powerful works of fables in mankind's set of experiences. These tales highlight humanized creatures as focal characters and pass ageless moral illustrations on through their activities and communications. Aesop's Tales enthrall perusers with their drawing in stories as well as act as a significant investigation of human instinct, morals, and cultural qualities. This paper digs into the universe of Aesop's Tales, looking at their starting points, the meaning of creature characters, and the getting through illustrations they keep on conferring to perusers, everything being equal.

The Starting points and Tradition of Aesop's Tales

Aesop, the unbelievable figure credited with the making of these tales, is accepted to have lived in antiquated Greece around the sixth century BCE. Albeit the authentic presence of Aesop is covered in legend, his impact on narrating and moral guidance is obviously significant.

The stories credited to him were at first passed down orally, with every age adding its own varieties and translations. In the long run, these tales were kept recorded as a hard copy, turning into a loved piece of worldwide fables.

Aesop's Tales are described by their brief narrating, sharp mind, and adroit moral illustrations. They cover a large number of subjects, including insight, keenness, modesty, trustworthiness, and the outcomes of one's activities. Regardless of being established in old Greek culture, the general allure of Aesop's Tales rises above time and social limits. These accounts have been converted into various dialects and keep on being adjusted, reevaluated, and appreciated by individuals all over the planet.

The Meaning of Creature Characters in Aesop's Tales

Vital to the persevering through allure of Aesop's Tales are the creature characters that populate these stories. Through the humanoid attribution of creatures, Aesop gives an interesting and drawing in system for conveying moral examples. The utilization of creatures as characters fills a few urgent needs:

Appeal: Creatures have natural ways of behaving, attributes, and senses that are unmistakable to people. By ascribing human-like characteristics to creatures, Aesop makes the ethical illustrations open and appealing to perusers, everything being equal.

Comprehensiveness: Creature conduct and attributes are general, rising above social and semantic obstructions. Accordingly, the ethical illustrations passed on through creature characters reverberate with assorted crowds around the world.

Objectivity: Creatures, without complex human feelings and cultural settings, give an objective focal point through which to look at moral problems and moral decisions. This permits perusers to zero in on the center illustrations without getting trapped in unambiguous social or verifiable settings.

Moral story and Imagery: The creature characters in Aesop's Tales act as symbolic portrayals of human characteristics and ways of behaving. For instance, the shrewdness fox might address double dealing, while the savvy owl encapsulates intelligence. This metaphorical methodology takes into account layered understandings and more profound reflections on human instinct.

Key Topics and Profound quality Examples in Aesop's Tales

Aesop's Tales cover many topics, offering significant experiences into human way of behaving, morals, and cultural qualities. A portion of the vital topics and the illustrations they confer include:

The Results of Misdirection and Eagerness:

"The Kid Who Told a shameful lie": This notable tale cautions against untrustworthiness and the results of misleading problems. It shows the significance of validity and the risks of double dealing.

"The Canine and Its Appearance": This tale features the indiscretion of voracity and the risks of overextending. The canine loses the bone it previously had while attempting to snatch the reflected bone, showing the illustration that it is smarter to be happy with what one has.

Insight and Sly:

"The Fox and the Grapes": This tale investigates the idea of harsh grapes, representing how people legitimize their disappointments or unfulfilled cravings. It cautions against self-trickery and the risks of excusing what one can't achieve.

"The Turtle and the Rabbit": This notorious tale stresses the worth of steadiness and modesty. The gradual turtle at last victories over the careless and smug bunny, instructing that predictable exertion prompts achievement.

The Risks of Excessive smugness:

"The Vast majority": This tale alerts against eagerness and gaudiness. The lion's endeavor to guarantee the whole crown jewels prompts a debate with different creatures, highlighting the risks of extreme pride.

The Ideals of Collaboration and Solidarity:

"The Heap of Sticks": This tale outlines the strength that comes from solidarity. The example is that people are more grounded together, accentuating the significance of collaboration and cooperation.

"The Rancher and His Children": This tale shows the worth of family solidarity and the significance of cooperating for a long term benefit.

The Force of Thoughtfulness and Sympathy:

"The Lion and the Mouse": This tale shows the way that little thoughtful gestures can have huge results. The mouse's demonstration of empathy towards the lion at last prompts a day to day existence saving blessing consequently.

The Risks of Rash Decisions:

"The Ass' Shadow": This tale alerts against making hurried decisions disregarding the full setting. The silliness of pursuing an incomprehensible shadow features the risks of indiscreet choices.

The Imprudence of Jealousy and Examination:

"The Ass and the Lapdog": This tale cautions against begrudging the conditions of others. The silly ass, craving the spoiled existence of the lapdog, at last loses its opportunity and autonomy.

The Persevering through Pertinence of Aesop's Tales

The persevering through significance of Aesop's Tales lies in their capacity to distil complex moral and moral examples into available and drawing in accounts. Their widespread subjects and engaging creature characters permit perusers, everything being equal, to gather important bits of knowledge into human way of behaving and cultural qualities. Also, Aesop's Tales have risen above time and keep on reverberating with contemporary crowds in light of multiple factors:

Agelessness: The ethical examples conveyed in these tales are immortal, tending to central parts of human way of behaving and morals. The topics of genuineness, shrewdness, modesty, and thoughtfulness stay as pertinent today as they were in antiquated Greece.

Versatility: Aesop's Tales are versatile to different settings and crowds. They can be utilized to show kids significant life examples, act as prompts for philosophical conversations, or be incorporated into instructive educational plans.

Multifaceted Allure: The general subjects investigated in these tales make them open to individuals from different social foundations. They give a shared belief to examining moral situations and human instinct.

Multifaceted Translations: Aesop's Tales are complex accounts that welcome perusers to dive into more profound understandings. The metaphorical idea of the creature characters takes into consideration nuanced conversations of human characteristics and ways of behaving.

Social Editorial: These tales frequently act as a type of social discourse, scrutinizing cultural qualities and ways of behaving. They urge perusers to think about their own decisions and decisions considering the examples introduced.

Consistent Variation: Aesop's Tales keep on being adjusted into different types of media, from youngsters' books and vivified movies to theater and workmanship. Their persevering through ubiquity guarantees that new ages are presented to their insight.

Moral Contemplations and Contemporary Points of view

While Aesop's Tales offer important moral direction, they are not without analysis and moral contemplations, especially when seen through contemporary points of view. A few worries include:

Oversimplified Perspective: Aesop's Tales present an improved visible of profound quality, which may not address the intricacies and subtleties of genuine moral issues. Pundits contend that the obvious illustrations may not enough plan people for the complexities of present day moral direction.

Generalizing: A few tales contain generalizations and predispositions, sustaining negative pictures of specific creature characters. These generalizations can stretch out to human gatherings when applied figuratively, possibly supporting biased sees.

Absence of Social Variety: Aesop's Tales dominatingly mirror the social and social setting of old Greece. They may not sufficiently address the different viewpoints and upsides of contemporary worldwide social orders.

Adjusting the immortal insight of Aesop's Tales with contemporary moral contemplations includes involving these tales as a beginning stage for conversations instead of depending on them as prescriptive aides. It is fundamental to empower decisive reasoning, moral investigation, and a comprehension of the intricacies of present day profound quality.

7.2 Beast Epics in World Literature

Monster sagas, a particular classification inside world writing, offer enamoring stories that include creatures as focal characters. These amazing stories, frequently established in old oral practices, investigate the perplexing connections among people and creatures while conveying significant examples, cultural scrutinizes, and immortal insight. From the beginning of time, different societies all over the planet have embraced monster sagas, winding around rich embroideries of stories where creatures act as metaphorical, human, and representative figures. This article dives into the universe of monster legends, investigating their starting points, key qualities, and persevering through impact in world writing.

The Starting points of Monster Sagas

Monster legends have old starting points that can be followed back to oral narrating customs, making them a critical piece of human scholarly legacy. These stories, passed down from one age to another, frequently advanced because of social, cultural, and natural changes. While the beginnings of explicit monster sagas are assorted and mind boggling, the absolute most remarkable models include:

Indian Monster Sagas: Indian writing flaunts two prestigious monster stories - the Panchatantra and the Jataka stories. The Panchatantra, created around 200 BCE, highlights creature characters that confer moral and useful insight through metaphorical accounts. The Jataka stories, beginning from the Buddhist custom, describe the past existences of the Buddha, frequently with creatures as heroes.

African Monster Stories: African oral customs are packed with monster sagas that utilization creatures as characters to convey social insight and lessons. Anansi the bug, Rabbit, and Lion are repeating creature figures in these stories. They frequently investigate subjects of mind, tricky, and shared values.

Archaic European Monster Stories: In middle age Europe, monster legends like "Reynard the Fox" and "Isengrim the Wolf" were well known accounts that introduced creatures as symbolic figures. "Reynard the Fox," specifically, scrutinized and ridiculed human culture, offering a mirror to the flaws and indecencies of the human world.

Antiquated Greek and Roman Monster Tales: Aesop's Tales, albeit known for their more limited, moralistic accounts, additionally fall inside the domain of monster stories. These stories highlight creatures as human characters and proposition illustrations in shrewdness, profound quality, and social way of behaving.

Old Chinese Monster Stories: The Chinese practice incorporates the "Excursion toward the West," an exemplary novel that includes a wide cluster of creature and otherworldly characters. This epic portrays the undertakings of the Monkey Ruler and his mates, drawing from Taoist, Buddhist, and Confucian ways of thinking.

Key Attributes of Monster Legends

Monster sagas share a few key qualities that recognize them as a classification inside world writing:

Humanoid attribution: Monster stories frequently utilize humanoid attribution, supplying creatures with human-like characteristics, ways of behaving, and qualities. This permits the creature characters to participate in complex social and moral situations, reflecting human encounters and feelings.

Purposeful anecdote and Imagery: Creature characters in monster stories frequently capability as metaphorical or emblematic figures. They address human characteristics, cultural qualities, excellencies, indecencies, and moral illustrations. The activities and communications of these creatures convey more profound implications past their strict jobs.

Moral and Moral Examples: Monster sagas are prestigious for granting moral and moral illustrations through their accounts. These stories act for the purpose of conveying intelligence, cultural qualities, and down to earth direction. They urge perusers to ponder the illustrations inside the tales and apply them to their own lives.

Complex Topics: Monster sagas investigate a different scope of subjects, including intelligence, sly, ethicalness, bad habit, equity, and the outcomes of one's activities. These topics frequently mirror the human condition and cultural elements.

Study and Parody: Some monster stories, similar to "Reynard the Fox," capability as mocking and basic accounts that evaluate human culture and its blemishes. They utilize creatures as heroes to uncover human shortcomings and weaknesses.

Versatility: Monster legends are versatile accounts that can be reevaluated in different social settings. They keep on moving transformations in writing, theater, workmanship, and different types of media.

Prominent Monster Stories from Around the World

The universe of monster sagas is rich and various, with each culture contributing its own one of a kind stories. The absolute most outstanding models include:

"Panchatantra" (India): The "Panchatantra," frequently alluded to as the Indian Aesop's Tales, is an assortment of stories highlighting creature characters. These stories pass functional and moral insight on through figurative accounts. The tales investigate subjects of kinship, shrewdness, and clever.

"Reynard the Fox" (Middle age Europe): "Reynard the Fox" is a praised monster epic that started in archaic Europe. The account rotates around Reynard, the finesse fox, who utilizes his mind and shrewdness to outfox different creature characters. The legendary fills in as an ironical discourse on the imperfections of human culture.

"The Excursion toward the West" (China): "Excursion toward the West," an exemplary of Chinese writing, includes a plenty of creature and otherworldly characters setting out on a journey. The Monkey Lord, Sun Wukong, is a conspicuous figure who addresses both naughtiness and edification. The story draws from Taoist, Buddhist, and Confucian methods of reasoning.

"The Monster Epic of Balarama" (India): This less popular Indian monster epic recounts the account of Balarama, the senior sibling of Ruler Krishna. It includes the experiences of Balarama as he experiences different creatures and legendary animals. The story is saturated with social and strict imagery.

"The Joke artist Stories" (African Oral Customs): African oral practices swarm with monster sagas that element characters like Anansi the insect, Bunny, and Lion. These stories frequently focus on the intelligence of these characters and their capacity to outsmart others.

The Persevering through Impact of Monster Legends

Monster sagas have made a permanent imprint on world writing and keep on impacting narrating and social customs. Their getting through allure can be credited to a few elements:

Widespread Topics: Monster stories investigate all inclusive subjects and moral difficulties that resound with individuals across different societies and time spans. The illustrations they pass are ageless and pertinent on to different parts of the human experience.

Multi-layered Translations: The figurative and emblematic nature of monster sagas takes into account diverse understandings. Perusers can investigate the accounts on various levels, diving into the ethical examples, social editorial, and social imagery.

Social Character: Monster stories are necessary to social personality, mirroring the qualities, convictions, and perspectives of various social orders. They are a method for saving and communicating social legacy.

Abstract Variations: Monster legends have propelled endless artistic transformations, from novel retellings to shows. These transformations revive the stories, guaranteeing that they stay open and connecting with to contemporary crowds.

Moral Reflection: Monster stories support moral reflection and thought. Perusers are incited to consider the illustrations inside the tales and how they connect with their own lives and moral decisions.

Moral Contemplations and Present day Points of view

While monster stories offer significant bits of knowledge into profound quality and human way of behaving, they are not without moral contemplations. A portion of the worries related with these stories include:

Generalizing and Inclination: Monster stories might contain generalizations or predispositions, possibly propagating negative pictures of specific creature characters or human gatherings. Moral perusers ought to move toward these accounts basically and think about their verifiable and social settings.

Developing Moral Principles: A few stories might contain components that are conflicting with current moral norms. Perusers ought to know about these distinctions and take part in conversations that think about contemporary points of view on profound quality and cultural qualities.

Social Assignment: Variations or understandings of monster legends by people from outside the starting society might raise worries of social allocation. Moving toward these stories with social awareness and regard for their origins is fundamental.

7.3 Lessons from Animal Narratives

Over the course of writing and narrating, creatures play had a critical impact as characters in stories. These creature characters, frequently humanized to have human-like characteristics, take part in many experiences, difficulties, and moral problems. Whether in tales, folktales, fantasies, or contemporary writing, creature accounts have furnished perusers with important life illustrations, moral bits of knowledge, and reflections on the human condition. This paper dives into the universe of creature stories, investigating the examples they grant and their getting through pertinence in writing and society.

The Rich Custom of Creature Stories

Creature stories have a rich and various custom that traverses various societies, districts, and verifiable periods. They act as a general and open mode for conveying intelligence and ethical quality. Probably the most conspicuous instances of creature stories include:

Aesop's Tales (Antiquated Greece): Aesop's Tales, ascribed to the old Greek narrator Aesop, are famous for their compact and moralistic accounts highlighting humanized creatures. These tales address different ideals, indecencies, and moral situations.

The Panchatantra (India): The Panchatantra, an old Indian assortment of creature tales, confers insight through the accounts of talking creatures. It investigates topics of discretion, fellowship, and crafty.

The Siblings Grimm Fantasies (Germany): The Siblings Grimm integrated creature characters into their well known fantasies. Stories like "The Wolf and the Seven Small children" and "Hansel and Gretel" use creatures to represent different moral examples.

African Legends: African fables is wealthy in creature stories, frequently highlighting characters like Anansi the bug, Rabbit, and Lion. These stories convey social qualities, authentic information, and moral lessons.

Contemporary Writing: In present day writing, creature stories keep on flourishing. Books like "Charlotte's Internet" by E.B. White and "Watership Down" by Richard Adams utilize creature characters to investigate subjects of fellowship, penance, and the pattern of life.

Examples from Creature Accounts

Creature stories offer a plenty of examples that touch upon different parts of life, morals, and human way of behaving. These examples are both immortal and general, and they keep on reverberating with perusers, everything being equal. A portion of the key illustrations include:

Moral and Moral Direction: Creature stories frequently act as moral and moral compasses. They guide perusers in pursuing highminded decisions and grasping the results of their activities. For instance, Aesop's Tales show the significance of genuineness, graciousness, and modesty.

Insight and Sly: Numerous creature accounts underscore the worth of intelligence and sly. Characters like the shrewd owl or the sharp fox show the way that astuteness and cleverness can prompt achievement, even in testing circumstances.

Sympathy and Sympathy: Creature stories every now and again feature the meaning of empathy and compassion. Accounts of creatures helping each other or offering grace to people urge perusers to think about the significance of these characteristics in their own lives.

Outcomes of Avarice and Narrow-mindedness: Eagerness and childishness are normal subjects in creature accounts. Characters who focus on their cravings over the prosperity of others frequently face adverse results. These accounts highlight the significance of sharing and benevolence.

Steadiness and Assurance: Creature stories frequently include characters who face affliction earnestly and persistence. These accounts motivate perusers to remain focused on their objectives and to defeat difficulties.

The Force of Fellowship and Collaboration: Companionship and participation are repeating topics in creature stories. Characters cooperating to accomplish shared objectives exhibit the strength of solidarity and coordinated effort.

Results of Misdirection and Unscrupulousness: Duplicity and deceitfulness are focal topics in numerous creature accounts. Characters that untruth or misdirect others frequently face adverse results, underscoring the significance of trustworthiness and honesty.

Flexibility and Versatility: Creatures in these accounts frequently show strength and flexibility while confronting troublesome conditions. These characteristics motivate perusers to embrace change and defeat difficulty in their own lives.

Persevering through Pertinence of Creature Accounts

The getting through significance of creature accounts can be credited to a few variables:

Ageless Subjects: The topics investigated in creature accounts, like genuineness, thoughtfulness, and astuteness, are immortal and keep on being important in contemporary society. These accounts offer persevering through intelligence and moral direction.

Availability: Creature stories are open to perusers of any age and foundations. Their straightforwardness and appeal make them significant devices for showing values and morals.

Diverse Understandings: Creature accounts frequently contain numerous layers of significance. Youngsters might see the value in the superficial story, while grown-ups can dive into more profound understandings and philosophical conversations.

All inclusiveness: Creature accounts are generally interesting. The encounters and feelings of creatures in these accounts reflect human encounters, permitting perusers from assorted foundations to associate with the characters.

Versatility: These accounts are versatile and keep on rousing variations in different types of media, including film, theater, and craftsmanship. Their persevering through request guarantees that they stay available to new ages.

Challenges and Moral Contemplations

While creature accounts offer important examples and bits of knowledge, they are not without their difficulties and moral contemplations. A few worries include:

Social Awareness: A few creature stories might contain social components or generalizations that can be inhumane or improper. Moving toward these accounts with social responsiveness and awareness is fundamental.

Developing Moral Norms: A few stories might contain components that don't line up with present day moral principles. Perusers ought to know about these distinctions and participate in conversations that think about contemporary points of view on ethical quality and cultural qualities.

Social Assignment: Transformations or understandings of creature stories by people from outside the beginning society might raise worries of social allotment. Moving toward these stories with deference for their origins is significant.

Chapter 8

Myths, Ecology, and Conservation

Fantasies play had a significant impact in forming the manner in which people see and cooperate with the regular world. They frequently act as a focal point through which environmental and preservation issues are perceived. This 3000-word exposition investigates the complicated connection between legends, biology, and preservation. We will dig into the manners by which legends have affected human associations with the climate, look at how biological comprehension has educated the creation regarding fantasies, and talk about what fantasies keep on significance for protection endeavors.

The Impact of Fantasies on Nature

Fantasies, since days of yore, have been utilized to make sense of regular peculiarities and the interconnectedness of every single living being. These accounts, frequently established in social and otherworldly convictions, assist people with figuring out their general surroundings and confer examples about their place in nature.

Quite possibly of the most widely recognized topic in fantasies is the idea of a "characteristic request" or a "equilibrium of nature." Numerous legends highlight tales about divine beings or spirits who control the components, creatures, and environments. For instance, in Greek folklore, Gaia was the Earth goddess who addressed the whole regular world. Her kids, the Titans, administered different parts of the climate, like the seas, backwoods, and mountains. These fantasies mirror a comprehension of the interconnectedness of natural frameworks and the possibility that upsetting this equilibrium can have desperate outcomes.

In Local American societies, legends frequently spin around the connection among people and creatures. The Navajo creation story, for example, accentuates the requirement for people to live as one with nature and regard the equilibrium of the world. This biological viewpoint is woven into the social texture, directing hunting, assembling, and land use rehearses.

Fantasies likewise assumed a part in molding social mentalities towards explicit species. The narrative of the phoenix, a legendary bird that ascents from its remains, represents restoration and interminability. Along these lines, the fantasy has added to how we might interpret recovery in biological systems and the significance of protecting territories for species' endurance. Different legends, like those about mythical beasts or snakes, could have filled in as clarifications for cataclysmic events like quakes, further underscoring the puzzling and frequently hazardous nature of the regular world.

While fantasies may not be founded on logical proof, they have given a moral and moral structure for grasping mankind's relationship with the climate. They frequently accentuate the results of biological bungle or the significance of living as one with nature. In that capacity, fantasies have molded human impression of the regular world, impacting our qualities, convictions, and activities.

The Biology of Legends

On the other side, biology has likewise added to the production of fantasies. As people contemplated and comprehend the normal world all the more profoundly, they drew upon their environmental information to create stories and fantasies.

One model is the legend of the "Leshy" in Slavic fables. The Leshy is a woodland soul that pulls pranks on voyagers and misleads them in the forest. Environmentally, this legend might have emerged as a method for making sense of the perplexing idea of thick timberlands, where one could undoubtedly get derailed without legitimate route abilities. It filled in as a wake up call, empowering individuals to regard the complexities of the backwoods and not underestimate nature.

Also, old's comprehension sailors might interpret sea flows and tides affected the making of fantasies about ocean beasts and slippery waters. These legends might have been utilized as admonitions to explore securely and stay away from risky regions.

In Local American societies, biological information was woven into fantasies as a method for passing down significant data about plants, creatures, and environments. These accounts frequently contained bits of knowledge about restorative plants, untamed life conduct, and occasional changes. They filled in as both instructive devices and social articulations, interfacing people to their regular environmental factors.

The Biology of Fantasies not just assisted with making sense of the secrets of the regular world yet in addition assumed a part in saving and sending natural insight starting with one age then onto the next. These legends were engaging as well as filled a commonsense need in passing on fundamental information for endurance.

Protection in the Cutting edge World

As human social orders developed and extended, our effects on the normal world developed dramatically. The Modern Unrest, the development of farming, and urbanization have prompted broad territory obliteration, contamination, and the overexploitation of regular assets. Preservation endeavors have arisen in light of these difficulties, meaning to save and safeguard the climate and its species.

While environmental information has progressed essentially, legends customary stories actually assume a part in protection. They can be utilized to rouse and draw in individuals in the protection of the normal world.

For instance, in present day ecological training, the narratives of jeopardized species and their battles for endurance are frequently imparted to the expectation of spurring people to make a move.

Fantasies and legends can likewise be bridled to make a feeling of spot and social personality connected to the climate. Native people group, specifically, have used their fantasies and oral practices to advocate for the preservation of their tribal terrains and the assurance of imperiled species. These accounts are a wellspring of social pride as well as an amazing asset for building support for preservation drives.

One outstanding illustration of this is the Haida nation of the Pacific Northwest, who have a rich oral practice and legends interweaved with the normal world. They have been effectively engaged with endeavors to moderate the old-development woodlands and safeguard the territory of the Northern Goshawk, a types of incredible social importance. The fantasies of the Haida public feature the interconnectedness of their way of life, their property, and the species they are attempting to save.

Besides, the connection among folklore and protection reaches out to the more extensive public. Preservation associations frequently utilize narrating and legend making to interface with individuals on a profound level. The magnetic megafauna, like tigers, pandas, and elephants, have been mythologized in mainstream society, becoming images of protection endeavors. These species have caught the public's creative mind and earned help for preservation projects.

In writing and film, accounts of natural legends, as "FernGully: The Last Rainforest" and "Symbol," have carried biological issues to a standard crowd. These stories stress the interconnectedness of all life and the need to safeguard the climate. While fictitious, they rouse true preservation endeavors and natural activism.

Accommodating Fantasies and Science in Protection

Protection frequently depends on logical information and research to illuminate direction. While legends play a fundamental part to play in motivating and drawing in individuals in protection, they should be accommodated with logical comprehension. This coordination is essential for viable protection systems.

For instance, the fantasy of the "Bigfoot" or "Yeti" has caught the well known creative mind and prompted various campaigns and looks for this amazing animal. While the presence of such an animal remaining parts unverified by logical proof, the interest in Bigfoot has unintentionally caused to notice the distant wild regions where it is said to stay. Progressives can utilize this interest with the fantasy to advance the insurance of these wild living spaces and the species that occupy them, regardless of whether Bigfoot itself stays slippery.

Protection associations can team up with native networks to overcome any issues between customary environmental information and logical exploration. Native people groups' profound comprehension of their neighborhood environments, frequently implanted in their legends and oral customs, can offer important experiences for preservation rehearses. By joining this native insight with logical techniques, more compelling protection systems can be created.

Fantasies and Legends in Current Preservation Drives

Numerous contemporary preservation drives integrate fantasies, legends, and social stories to make a feeling of association among individuals and the climate. These drives perceive the force of these stories to move change and impart a feeling of obligation for the normal world.

The White Stork Venture: In Europe, the White Stork Undertaking has attempted to once again introduce white storks to their verifiable favorable places. White storks are related with fantasies and legends all through Europe, frequently representing best of luck and ripeness. By restoring these social associations, the task expects to advance stork preservation and draw in nearby networks in safeguarding their natural surroundings.

The Narrative of the Kakapo: The kakapo, a basically imperiled parrot from New Zealand, has turned into a significant species in preservation endeavors. The tale of Sirocco, a charming kakapo who turned into a worldwide sensation through viral recordings and narratives, delineates how a solitary individual can catch the world's consideration and produce support for protection. Sirocco's story turned into a cutting edge fantasy, helping bring issues to light and assets for kakapo recuperation endeavors.

The Arrival of the California Condor: The California condor, one of the world's most jeopardized birds, has been brought back from the verge of eradication through a cooperative recuperation program. The condor holds social importance to numerous native people groups in the American West, and their fantasies and customs play had an impact in the bird's protection. By regarding these social associations and integrating them into the recuperation program, progressives have accumulated help and commitment from neighborhood networks.

Legendary Animals in Marine Preservation: The making of marine safeguarded regions (MPAs) frequently includes the distinguishing proof of alluring species as leader species for protection endeavors. These species, like whales, dolphins, or ocean turtles, act as advanced fantasies, charming people in general and revitalizing help for the security of whole biological systems.

In these and numerous different cases, fantasies and legends have been tackled to make close to home associations among individuals and the regular world. These stories act as integral assets for connecting with the general population and collecting support for protection drives.

The Job of Fantasy in Tending to Protection Difficulties

Preservation faces various difficulties in the cutting edge world, from living space misfortune and environmental change to species eradication and contamination.

Fantasies and legends can assume a fundamental part in tending to these difficulties in more than one way.

Molding Public Discernment: Fantasies can shape public insight and impact perspectives toward preservation. Stories that underline the significance of safeguarding biodiversity, relieving environmental change, and safeguarding regular living spaces can urge individuals to make a move.

Bringing issues to light: Fantasies and legends can be utilized to bring issues to light about unambiguous protection issues. For instance, the tale of the legendary "ice bear" (polar bear) in Inuit culture is a powerful image of the Cold's weakness to environmental change. By sharing this story, the situation of polar bears turns out to be more interesting to the more extensive public.

Social Significance: Fantasies and legends are well established in social practices. Protection endeavors that regard and consolidate these accounts are bound to be embraced by neighborhood networks, especially native people groups, whose qualities and convictions are entwined with the climate.

Building a Feeling of obligation: Legends frequently convey moral examples. By associating biological issues to moral standards implanted in these accounts, progressives can move a feeling of obligation for the climate and its occupants.

8.1 Indigenous Wisdom and Environmental Ethics

Native people groups all over the planet have kept a profound and personal association with the climate for millennia. Their societies, customs, and perspectives are grounded in the insight of living as one with the regular world. This exposition investigates the crossing point of Native insight and natural morals, revealing insight into the significant bits of knowledge that Native societies proposition to address the worldwide ecological difficulties we face today.

Native Insight: An All encompassing Relationship with Nature

Native insight envelops a complicated snare of information, values, and practices that are well established in the land. The lessons of Native societies are much of the time elapsed down through oral practices, stories, and customs, underscoring an agreeable relationship with nature. Key components of Native insight include:

Hallowed Association: Native people groups see the regular world as consecrated and have confidence in the interconnectedness of every single living being. This interconnectedness is at the center of their otherworldly convictions, making a significant regard for nature and a feeling of obligation to safeguard it.

Supportability Practices: Native people group have created feasible practices that are finely tuned to their nearby biological systems. These practices incorporate regenerative farming, mindful hunting and fishing, and moral land the executives. The standards of supportability and stewardship have been fundamental to their lifestyle for ages.

Customary Environmental Information (TEK): Native societies have an abundance of conventional natural information, gave over through ages. This information incorporates the way of behaving of plants and creatures, occasional changes, atmospheric conditions, and the restorative properties of neighborhood verdure. TEK is an important asset for understanding and overseeing environments economically.

Otherworldliness and Animism: Numerous Native societies practice animism, accepting that all that in nature has a soul or cognizance. This conviction encourages a significant feeling of obligation towards the climate, as hurting nature is viewed as an attack against the spirits occupying it.

Shared Direction: Native social orders frequently take part in mutual dynamic cycles, underscoring aggregate prosperity over individual addition. These practices reach out to the administration of normal assets, guaranteeing that ecological choices are made with the drawn out soundness of the biological system as a primary concern.

Native Ecological Morals

The ecological morals of Native societies are profoundly implanted in their lifestyle. These morals incorporate a bunch of moral rules that guide their cooperations with the regular world. Key parts of Native natural morals include:

Regard for All Life: Native morals focus on the regard and worship for all living things, perceiving the inborn worth of each living being. This adoration stretches out to creatures, plants, and, surprisingly, the actual components.

Intergenerational Obligation: Native societies underscore the significance of passing down a sound climate to people in the future. The activities of the present are seen as a heritage for the people who will come later, and the climate is treated as a legacy to be safeguarded.

Non-Obstruction: Numerous Native moral structures pressure the possibility of non-impedance or negligible mediation in nature. Human exercises shouldn't disturb the regular request, and assets ought to be gathered with care and as per the natural equilibrium.

Correspondence: Native ecological morals frequently focus on the standard of correspondence. This implies rewarding the land and recognizing that people are essential for a mind boggling trap of connections. At the point when assets are taken, something of equivalent or more prominent worth should be offered as a trade off, like articulations of appreciation or preservation endeavors.

Preservation and Manageability: Native morals focus on the protection and maintainable utilization of regular assets. Rehearses like harvest pivot, controlled consumes, and rotational brushing are instances of the well established Native obligation to keeping up with the equilibrium of environments.

The Versatility of Native Insight

Regardless of hundreds of years of colonization, underestimation, and social disintegration, Native insight and natural morals have exhibited amazing versatility. Native people group have confronted a large number of difficulties, from dispossession of their territories to loss of social character, yet they keep on maintaining their ecological qualities and information frameworks. This strength is established in the acknowledgment of the basic association between social endurance and ecological prosperity.

Native people groups' opposition and strength are apparent in their endeavors to recover command over their tribal terrains, safeguard sacrosanct destinations, and renew their dialects and social practices. As they affirm their privileges and recover their social legacy, they frequently lead the way in advancing economical ecological practices and moral stewardship of the land.

Contextual analyses in Native Natural Morals

Maori Preservation Practices in New Zealand: The Maori nation of New Zealand have a profound association with their familial terrains and a solid obligation to protection. Through social practices like kaitiakitanga, and that implies guardianship, they play had a critical impact in reestablishing and safeguarding their common habitat. Drives like the Whanganui Stream being conceded legitimate personhood, recognizing its freedoms as a living element, mirror the combination of Native insight and present day lawful structures.

Navajo Ideas of Equilibrium and Concordance: The Navajo Country in the US accentuates the idea of Hózhǫ́, which means equilibrium and amicability in their natural morals. This idea is profoundly imbued in their way of life and guides their way to deal with asset the executives and natural protection. The Navajo Country has attempted ventures to reestablish and safeguard their territories, building up their obligation to keeping up with the fragile equilibrium of nature.

Inuit Hunting Customs in the Icy: The Inuit of the Cold have a long history of feasible hunting rehearses. They depend on a profound comprehension of the creatures they chase and have created explicit hunting morals that regard the respectability of the environment. For instance, the Inuit intently follow shares for reaping marine warm blooded creatures to guarantee the drawn out endurance of these species.

The Yoruba Public and Hallowed Forests: In Nigeria, the Yoruba public have laid out sacrosanct forests, like the Osun-Osogbo Consecrated Woods, as spaces of love and preservation. These forests act as safe-havens for novel biological systems, protecting biodiversity and exhibiting the combination of otherworldliness and ecological morals.

Native Commitments to Worldwide Ecological Morals

Native ecological morals offer important commitments to the more extensive worldwide natural talk. Here are a few manners by which their insight can improve our comprehension and guide our activities:

A Biocentric Point of view: Native morals challenge the human-centric view that places mankind at the focal point of moral thought. All things considered, they stress a biocentric viewpoint that esteems all living things and recognizes their inherent worth.

Long haul Maintainability: Native practices show a guarantee to long haul manageability and the conservation of biological systems for people in the future.

This approach diverges from the transient abuse of assets frequently found in current industrialized social orders.

Local area Based Direction: Native administration models energize mutual navigation, which can encourage aggregate liability regarding the climate and backing the advancement of earth sound approaches.

Association with Spot: Native societies' profound association with their hereditary grounds features the significance of spot based morals and supports the idea that the climate is certainly not a theoretical idea yet an unmistakable and hallowed piece of life.

Comprehensive Perspective: Native societies frequently advance an all encompassing perspective that perceives the interconnectedness of every single living being and the climate. This point of view can motivate a more far reaching and coordinated way to deal with resolving ecological issues.

Difficulties and Amazing open doors

While Native insight and natural morals offer significant experiences and answers for the present ecological difficulties, a few obstructions should be recognized and tended to:

Social Underestimation: Native people group have for some time been minimized and persecuted, which has frequently brought about the sabotaging of their natural practices and conventional information. Recognizing their privileges and supporting their self-assurance is fundamental.

Dangers to Conventional Terrains: Land dispossession and asset extraction compromise the capacity of Native people group to keep up with their customary practices and natural morals. Perceiving land freedoms and it is essential to protect their domains.

Social Allocation: The assignment of Native information and practices by non-Native substances can be manipulative and rude. Endeavors ought to be made to guarantee that Native insight is partaken in a socially delicate and deferential way.

Cooperation and Regard: Successful joint effort among Native and non-Native people group is critical to bridling the advantages of Native insight. Such coordinated effort should be founded on regard, assent, and fair organizations.

8.2 Animals in Modern Ecology and Conservation Movements

Creatures have forever been fundamental to environment and protection developments. From the spearheading work of naturalists like Charles Darwin and Alfred Russel Wallace to the foundation of safeguarded regions and untamed life safe-havens, creatures play had a significant impact in forming how we might interpret the normal world and rousing endeavors to safeguard it. This exposition dives into the connection among creatures and present day nature and protection developments, looking at their jobs as signs of ecological wellbeing, cornerstone species, and magnetic ministers for biodiversity preservation.

Marks of Ecological Wellbeing

Creatures act as crucial signs of natural wellbeing. Their populace elements, conduct, and physiological reactions can give significant experiences into the state of environments. Understanding these pointers is basic for evaluating the effect of human exercises and environmental change on the regular world.

Bioindicators: A few creatures, known as bioindicators, are especially delicate to ecological changes. For instance, creatures of land and water, like frogs and lizards, are frequently utilized as bioindicators on the grounds that their penetrable skin makes them profoundly defenseless to natural impurities. The decay of land and water proficient populaces can flag issues with water quality and other biological issues.

Birds as Ecological Sentinels: Birds are great natural sentinels because of their versatility, moderately lengthy life expectancies, and different living space inclinations. Ornithologists screen bird populaces to measure the strength of biological systems. For instance, decreases in specific bird species might demonstrate natural surroundings misfortune, contamination, or other environmental aggravations.

Pointer Species for Water Quality: Macroinvertebrates like mayflies, caddisflies, and stoneflies are utilized to survey water quality in freshwater environments. Their presence and variety demonstrate the biological honesty of streams and waterways. In regions with high contamination levels, the shortfall of these species is an obvious indicator of crumbling water quality.

Coral Reefs and Marine Biodiversity: Coral reefs are frequently alluded to as the "rainforests of the ocean" because of their staggering biodiversity. The presence or nonattendance of specific reef-abiding species can be utilized to evaluate the strength of these delicate environments. The mass dying occasions influencing coral reefs are obvious tokens of the outcomes of environmental change for marine life.

Vertebrates and Environmental Change: Warm blooded animals, especially those living in polar locales, are significant marks of environmental change influences. The decreasing populaces of polar bears, for example, act as an advance notice indication of the emotional impacts of an unnatural weather change on Icy environments.

Cornerstone Species and Trophic

Creatures are marks of natural wellbeing as well as key members in biological cycles. A few animal types, known as cornerstone species, assume outsized parts in keeping up with environment soundness and variety. The deficiency of these species can set off trophic fountains, prompting biological lopsided characteristics.

The Ocean Otter: The ocean otter, a cornerstone animal groups in kelp timberland environments, assumes an essential part in controlling ocean imp populaces. Without ocean otters, ocean imps overgraze kelp, prompting the corruption of kelp backwoods and the deficiency of natural surroundings for various marine species. The renewed introduction of ocean otters in certain areas has reestablished the equilibrium of these biological systems.

Wolves and Yellowstone Public Park: Dim wolves, once extirpated from Yellowstone Public Park, were once again introduced during the 1990s. Their presence prompted an outpouring of biological impacts, remembering a diminishing for the elk populace, permitting willow and aspen trees to recover. This, thusly, helped beavers, larks, and other natural life.

African Elephants and Savannas: African elephants, through their perusing and scavenging exercises, impact the design and structure of savanna biological systems. Their presence forestalls the infringement of woody vegetation, keeping up with open fields and helping a great many animal categories, from nibblers to hunters.

Hunters and Biodiversity: Hunters like large felines and raptors are in many cases cornerstone species in earthly biological systems. Their presence holds prey populaces under tight restraints, forestalling overgrazing and taking into consideration a more prominent variety of plant and creature species to coincide.

Honey bees and Fertilization: Numerous types of honey bees are fundamental pollinators for blossoming plants. Their job in fertilization guarantees the generation of various plant species, which, thus, give food and territory to a wide exhibit of creatures.

Charming Megafauna as Preservation Diplomats

Charming megafauna, huge and frequently notorious species, have caught the public's creative mind and assumed a critical part in preservation endeavors. These creatures act as ministers for biodiversity preservation, causing to notice bigger biological issues and moving activity.

The Goliath Panda: The monster panda has turned into a worldwide image of untamed life protection. These charming bears certainly stand out and subsidizing, helping their preservation as well as the insurance of their natural surroundings, which harbors incalculable different species.

The Bengal Tiger: The Bengal tiger is another alluring species that has drawn overall consideration. Protection endeavors to save the tiger have prompted the safeguarding of basic tiger territories, helping many different species having similar biological systems.

Marine Lead Species: Species like the humpback whale, ocean turtles, and extraordinary white sharks act as lead species for marine preservation. Their relocations and life narratives are convincing stories that bring issues to light about the significance of safeguarding marine biological systems and the requirement for maintainable fishing rehearses.

The African Elephant: African elephants are cornerstone species as well as magnetic megafauna. The ivory exchange and territory misfortune have seriously compromised elephant populaces, prompting worldwide preservation missions to safeguard them and their environments.

Wolves in North America: Wolves have been focal figures in protection discussions and missions, especially in North America. Their renewed introduction in Yellowstone Public Park featured the job of top hunters in keeping up with biological system balance and the significance of conjunction among people and untamed life.

Challenges in Preservation Endeavors

While alluring megafauna and cornerstone species assume imperative parts in preservation developments, they likewise present specific difficulties:

Imbalanced Needs: The attention on charming megafauna can now and again eclipse the significance of preserving less obvious species. A reasonable methodology is fundamental to guarantee the insurance of the whole biological system.

Single Species versus Biological systems: Protection endeavors focused on a solitary animal varieties might disregard the more extensive environmental setting in which that species lives. Environment based protection perceives the interconnectedness of all species and their territories.

Misinformed Public Discernment: Overemphasis on alluring species can prompt slanted public insights, where the destiny of less well known or less attractive species is neglected. This can influence subsidizing designation and asset distribution for preservation endeavors.

Struggle with People: The insurance of cornerstone species like wolves or huge hunters can prompt contentions with human exercises, for example, domesticated animals cultivating. Adjusting the requirements of individuals and untamed life is a complicated test in protection.

Misappropriation and Double-dealing: Magnetic megafauna can be taken advantage of for the travel industry, prompting adverse impacts on the species and their natural surroundings. Protection endeavors should zero in on mindful and reasonable the travel industry rehearses.

Protection Systems and Current Difficulties

Present day preservation endeavors perceive the significance of creatures as key parts of biological systems and the need to safeguard their living spaces. The accompanying methodologies and difficulties represent the continuous work in this field:

Safeguarded Regions and Natural surroundings Preservation: Laying out safeguarded regions and saving basic living spaces are essential protection methodologies. These regions give asylum to natural life and assist with keeping up with environmental cycles. In any case, the development of shielded regions can some of the time face resistance from human exercises and land use.

Natural life Hallways: Making natural life passageways or availability between divided territories is fundamental for species relocation and hereditary variety. Environmental change further highlights the significance of permitting species to move in light of moving natural surroundings.

Local area Based Preservation: Including nearby networks in protection endeavors is significant for long haul achievement. Perceiving the privileges and interests of native people groups and neighborhood networks in the administration of normal assets is fundamental for both biodiversity and human prosperity.

Hostage Reproducing and Renewed introduction: For basically jeopardized species, hostage rearing and renewed introduction programs are fundamental for their endurance. Notwithstanding, these projects accompany difficulties connected with hereditary variety, infection, and the variation of hostage creatures to nature.

Legitimate Systems and Peaceful accords: Peaceful accords and public regulations assume a fundamental part in the security of natural life and their living spaces. Arrangements like the Show on Worldwide Exchange Imperiled Species (Refers to) assist with controlling the exchange of jeopardized species and their items.

Environmental Change and Territory Movements: Environmental change represents a huge test to preservation endeavors. Creatures are now encountering territory moves and changes in their day to day existence cycles. Variation systems are vital for assist species with adapting to the evolving environment.

8.3 The Relevance of Animal Mythology in Contemporary Environmental Issues

All through mankind's set of experiences, creatures have been a basic piece of our folklore, fables, and social accounts. These creature fantasies have been utilized to make sense of normal peculiarities, convey moral examples, and give social character. In contemporary times, as we wrestle with squeezing natural issues, the importance of creature folklore becomes obvious. This paper investigates the manners by which creature folklore stays appropriate in tending to contemporary ecological difficulties. We will examine how fantasies can educate our comprehension regarding environmental frameworks, move protection endeavors, and act as an extension between customary thinking and current science.

The Social Meaning of Creature Folklore

Creature folklore is a fundamental piece of human culture and history. These legends frequently include creatures as focal characters, crediting them with human-like characteristics, powers, or characters. Creature fantasies serve a few significant social capabilities:

Making sense of Regular Peculiarities: In numerous antiquated societies, fantasies were utilized to make sense of the secrets of the normal world. For instance, the Norse creation fantasy recounts the world tree Yggdrasil, a debris tree whose roots stretch out into various domains of presence, and the extraordinary snake Níðhöggr that bites on its underlying foundations, representing the interconnectedness of all life and the pattern of creation and obliteration.

Showing Moral and Moral Examples: Creature legends frequently convey moral and moral illustrations. Aesop's tales, for example, highlight creatures as characters in stories that show excellencies, shrewdness, and life illustrations. The account of "The Turtle and the Rabbit" shows the worth of diligence and lowliness.

Social Personality and Imagery: Many societies use creatures as images that address their qualities, character, and association with the regular world. The bald eagle, for instance, is an image of opportunity and strength in American culture, while the lion addresses boldness and respectability in different African societies.

Customs and Customs: Creature legends are implanted in strict and social ceremonies. In Hindu folklore, the cow is venerated and thought about consecrated, prompting the practice of cow assurance in India.

The Job of Creature Folklore in Contemporary Natural Issues

In our advanced world, where ecological issues like environment misfortune, environmental change, and biodiversity misfortune compromise the normal world, the pertinence of creature folklore becomes apparent. These fantasies give significant bits of knowledge and motivation in tending to contemporary ecological difficulties.

Illuminating Biological Comprehension: Numerous creature fantasies contain components of environmental insight that can develop how we might interpret biological systems. The idea of the "web of life" or the interconnectedness of every single living being, frequently tracked down in creature fantasies, lines up with present day environmental comprehension. The acknowledgment that the soundness of one animal categories or living space is interconnected with others reverberates with contemporary ecological science.

Rousing Preservation Endeavors: Creature folklore can act as a wellspring of motivation for protection endeavors. Magnetic species highlighted in fantasies, similar to the lion, elephant, or falcon, frequently become meaningful of more extensive preservation crusades. These legendary animals, with their strong imagery, can mobilize backing and subsidizing for species and territory assurance.

Advancing Moral Stewardship: Creature legends oftentimes contain moral standards and illustrations about mankind's relationship with the normal world. These accounts underscore the significance of mindful stewardship and conjunction with the climate. Contemporary protection endeavors can draw from these moral lessons to encourage a feeling of obligation for the climate.

Spanning Customary Thinking and Present day Science: Creature folklore gives a scaffold between conventional biological information and current logical comprehension. Native societies, specifically, have a rich oral custom of creature fantasies that mirror their profound comprehension of nearby biological systems. Teaming up with native networks and integrating their customary thinking into preservation procedures can improve environmental reclamation and insurance endeavors.

The Insight of Creature Fantasies in Environmental Comprehension

Creature legends frequently contain natural insight that resounds with contemporary ecological science. These legends feature the interconnectedness of all life and the fragile equilibrium of biological systems.

The Fantasy of the White Bison: In Local American folklore, the white bison is viewed as a holy image of harmony and solidarity. The introduction of a white bison calf is viewed as a message of trust and compromise. Environmentally, this legend underscores the significance of safeguarding the normal world as a wellspring of solidarity and congruity.

The Turtle and the Bunny: Aesop's tale about the turtle and the rabbit shows the worth of constancy and slow, consistent advancement. With regards to natural issues, it underlines the requirement for reliable and supported preservation endeavors to conquer difficulties.

The Raven in Native Societies: The raven is a conspicuous figure in the folklore of numerous native societies, including the Local Americans of the Pacific Northwest and the native people groups of the Icy. The raven is many times depicted as a prankster figure, yet it likewise assumes a part in the formation of the world. Biologically, the raven's importance mirrors its versatility and cleverness in different environments, repeating the significance of flexibility despite ecological change.

The Rainforest Panther: In Focal and South American folklore, the puma is frequently connected with the rainforest and its many-sided trap of life. The panther is viewed as a gatekeeper of the backwoods and an image of security. Naturally, this legend highlights the job of top hunters in keeping up with biological system balance and the significance of saving their environments.

The Motivation of Creature Legends in Preservation Endeavors

Creature legends and their strong imagery have roused and informed preservation endeavors all over the planet. A portion of the manners by which these legends play had an impact in contemporary protection include:

The Lion in Preservation: The lion, frequently viewed as the ruler of the wilderness, is a significant species in African protection. The Maasai public, for instance, have areas of strength for an association with lions, seeing them as an image of solidarity and dauntlessness. Preservation associations have utilized this social importance to connect with neighborhood networks in lion protection endeavors.

The Thunderbird in Native Preservation: The Thunderbird is a noticeable figure in the folklore of numerous native societies in North America. It is frequently connected with downpour and the equilibrium of nature. Preservation drives including water and territory assurance have drawn on the imagery of the Thunderbird to advance ecological stewardship.

The Garuda in Southeast Asia: The Garuda, a legendary bird-like animal, is loved in Hindu and Buddhist folklore. This legendary animal has filled in as an image of social personality and ecological protection in Southeast Asian nations. Preservation endeavors in the district have utilized the imagery of the Garuda to bring issues to light and rouse activity.

The Mythical serpent in Asian Societies: In different Asian societies, the mythical beast is an image of force and security. Winged serpent legends have motivated preservation endeavors, especially connected with water asset the executives and security of amphibian biological systems. These endeavors line up with the mythical serpent's relationship with water and life.

The Moral Examples of Creature Fantasies for Ecological Stewardship

Creature fantasies frequently convey moral standards and examples about mankind's relationship with the normal world. These accounts stress the significance of mindful stewardship and conjunction with the climate.

Native Preservation Practices: Numerous native societies have created protection rehearses in light of the moral examples tracked down in their creature fantasies. These practices frequently include feasible hunting, fishing, and land the executives that focus on the prosperity of the climate and people in the future.

The Fantasy of the Phoenix: The phoenix, a legendary bird that is reawakened from its remains, represents recharging and eternality. This fantasy urges us to perceive the limit of environments to recuperate and recover whenever allowed the opportunity, stressing the significance of saving living spaces and biodiversity.

The Example of the Salmon: In native societies in North America and the Pacific Northwest, the existence pattern of the salmon is a focal subject in their folklore. The salmon's excursion from birth to generating and demise is a strong image of the pattern of life, penance, and recharging. This legend highlights the significance of safeguarding watersheds and guaranteeing the endurance of salmon populaces.

The Insight of the Owl: In many societies, owls are related with shrewdness and understanding. Owl fantasies feature the significance of understanding and regarding the normal world. This astuteness reaches out to protection works on, underscoring the requirement for educated and dependable natural choices.

The Extension Between Conventional Insight and Current Science

One of the critical commitments of creature folklore to contemporary natural issues is its capacity to connect customary biological information with current logical comprehension. Native societies, specifically, hold an abundance of environmental insight that is implanted in their legends and customs.

Native Information and Environment The board: Native people group have created unpredictable information frameworks about their neighborhood biological systems, frequently established in their legends and old stories. This information incorporates the way of behaving of creatures, the patterns of nature, and feasible asset the board rehearses. Working together with native networks can improve current preservation endeavors by drawing on their customary environmental information.

Nearby Environmental Insight: In different districts, neighborhood legends and stories contain bits of knowledge into the way of behaving of creatures, the planning of occasional occasions, and the connections between species. These experiences can illuminate biological examination and assist researchers with grasping complex natural frameworks.

Diverse Joint effort: Current preservation drives progressively perceive the worth of multifaceted cooperation. By drawing in with native networks and consolidating their customary thinking, progressives can improve the adequacy and manageability of their endeavors.

Difficulties and Contemplations

While the pertinence of creature folklore in contemporary natural issues is obvious, a few difficulties and contemplations should be recognized:

Social Responsiveness: Moving toward creature folklore with social awareness and respect is fundamental. Fantasies are well established in social personality and convictions, and they ought not be appropriated or misconstrued for preservation purposes.

Joining Customary Thinking with Science: The mix of conventional natural information with current science can challenge. Figuring out something worth agreeing on and laying out cooperative associations between native networks and protection associations demands investment, exertion, and common regard.

Different Viewpoints: There is no single general folklore or set of stories that apply to all societies. The preservation local area should perceive the variety of points of view and legends overall and move toward each culture with transparency and regard.

Adjusting Protection Needs: While alluring species and symbolic fantasies can be viable in motivating protection endeavors, they should be offset with the more extensive objective of biodiversity conservation. Preservation methodologies ought to think about the insurance of all species and biological systems.

Chapter 9

The Legacy of Animal Symbolism in Art, Literature, and Popular Culture

All through mankind's set of experiences, creatures have held an unmistakable spot in our aggregate creative mind, rousing workmanship, writing, and mainstream society. The utilization of creature imagery in these types of imaginative articulation is a demonstration of the getting through interest with the animals of the world collectively. This exposition investigates the tradition of creature imagery in different imaginative, artistic, and mainstream society settings, diving into the rich embroidery of implications and translations related with creatures and their portrayals.

The Meaning of Creature Imagery

Creature imagery has been an unavoidable and flexible topic in human culture for centuries. It has filled in for the purpose of communicating complex thoughts, feelings, and convictions through the language of representation and moral story. The meaning of creature imagery can be grasped in more than one way:

Social Signifiers: Creatures frequently act as social signifiers, addressing explicit characteristics, values, and convictions inside a general public. For example, the falcon is an image of opportunity in the US, while the mythical beast conveys different implications in Asian societies.

Figurative Understanding: Creatures much of the time show up in symbolic works, where they exemplify conceptual ideas or moral examples. Aesop's tales, for instance, highlight creatures as characters to convey moral lessons.

Prototype Implications: A few creatures, similar to the lion, the snake, or the owl, have model implications in human culture. These images are all inclusive and repetitive, rising above social limits and bringing out profound mental and close to home reactions.

Impression of the Regular World: Creature imagery frequently mirrors human-kind's relationship with the normal world. Creatures address our association with nature, our dependence on its assets, and our obligations as stewards of the climate.

The Tradition of Creature Imagery in Workmanship

Creature imagery has made a critical imprint on the universe of craftsmanship, with endless canvases, models, and other innovative works highlighting creatures as subjects and images. These works of art have left a significant inheritance, with different creature themes and imagery persevering as the centuries progressed.

Strict and Legendary Workmanship: Creatures assume a conspicuous part in strict and fanciful craftsmanship across societies. For instance, the Hindu god Ganesh is portrayed with the top of an elephant, representing intelligence and favorability. In Christian craftsmanship, the sheep frequently represents Christ's guiltlessness and penance.

Natural life Portrayal: Craftsmen have for some time been roused by the regular world, delivering similar portrayals of creatures. John James Audubon's "Birds of America" is an exemplary illustration of ornithological workmanship that exhibits the magnificence and variety of avian life.

Symbolist Workmanship: The Symbolist craftsmanship development of the late nineteenth century investigated subjects of the oblivious and the otherworldly using images, including creatures. Gustave Moreau's "The Spirit" and Odilon Redon's "The Cyclops" are instances of works that utilized creature imagery to inspire mysterious and fanciful characteristics.

Surrealist Workmanship: Oddity, a twentieth century craftsmanship development, frequently consolidated fanciful and fantastical components, including creature imagery. Salvador Dalí's "The Elephants" and René Magritte's "The Misleading Mirror" are outstanding models.

The Tradition of Creature Imagery in Writing

Creature imagery is similarly pervasive in writing, from old legends to contemporary books. Writers have utilized creatures to address many thoughts and subjects, giving perusers layers of understanding and knowledge.

Aesop's Tales: Aesop's tales, tracing all the way back to old Greece, are an assortment of brief tales that highlight creatures as characters, each delineating an ethical illustration. These tales have been broadly perused and adjusted into different societies, giving ageless insight through creature imagery.

Animal Homestead by George Orwell: In "Animal Ranch," George Orwell utilizes a cast of livestock to mock political frameworks and human way of behaving. The story involves creatures as figurative portrayals of political figures, for example, the pig Napoleon representing Joseph Stalin.

Moby-Dick by Herman Melville: "Moby-Dick" involves the whale as a focal image, addressing both nature's greatness and its disastrous power. The story investigates subjects of fixation, the human relationship with the regular world, and the quest for tricky bits of insight.

Watership Somewhere near Richard Adams: "Watership Down" is an undertaking novel including a gathering of bunnies and their mission for another home. The hares are something other than creatures; they epitomize complex characters with their own societies and social orders, showing topics of gallantry, authority, and the human condition.

The Tradition of Creature Imagery in Mainstream society

Creatures have likewise assumed a huge part in molding mainstream society. From enlivened characters to mascots, creatures have become notorious figures that resound with crowds around the world. The following are a couple of instances of creature imagery in mainstream society:

Mickey Mouse and Disney Characters: Mickey Mouse, made by Walt Disney, is one of the most unmistakable and adored fictitious people around the world. Disney's humanized creature characters, like Simba from "The Lion Lord" and Baloo from "The Wilderness Book," have resounded with ages, conveying moral and close to home illustrations.

Sports Mascots: Many games groups include creature mascots, frequently picked for their characteristics and properties. For instance, the Chicago Bulls mascot represents strength and assurance, while the Atlanta Falcons mascot typifies quickness and deftness.

Promoting Symbols: Publicizing oftentimes utilizes creature imagery to pass on brand messages and associate with shoppers. The Geico gecko addresses a well disposed and congenial insurance agency, while the Catalyst Rabbit represents perseverance and dependable energy.

Web Images: modern times has brought about innumerable creature themed images, from Irritable Feline to Doge. These creature images are frequently diverting and act as vehicles for parody, discourse, and social references.

The Diverse Translations of Creature Imagery

The persevering through tradition of creature imagery in craftsmanship, writing, and mainstream society lies in its ability for diverse translations. Creatures are rich images that can convey a large number of implications, frequently at the same time. A portion of the common topics and understandings of creature imagery include:

Model Images: Certain creatures, similar to the bird, the lion, or the snake, have profound prototype implications that have persevered through societies and times. The lion, for instance, is an image of solidarity, boldness, and respectability, frequently used to address the two people and countries.

Moral Purposeful anecdote: Creature imagery is much of the time utilized to convey moral illustrations and moral standards. Aesop's tales are an exemplary illustration of how creatures exemplify temperances, indecencies, and life examples. The fox might represent clever, while the turtle addresses persistence and assurance.

Social Signifiers: Creatures act as social signifiers, addressing explicit qualities and personalities. In Chinese culture, the winged serpent is related with power and security, while the panda represents harmony and tact.

Ecological Messages: Creature imagery frequently mirrors humankind's relationship with the normal world. The predicament of jeopardized species, like the polar bear, can act as images of natural protection and environmental change mindfulness.

Political Editorial: Creatures are often utilized in political parody and discourse. George Orwell's "Animal Homestead" is a great representation of how creatures can represent political figures and frameworks.

Individual and Mental Translations: Creature images can likewise hold individual importance for people. An individual might relate to a specific creature in light of its characteristics and qualities, involving it as a symbol or seal.

Contemporary Significance and Translation

The significance of creature imagery in contemporary culture is unmistakable. In a quickly impacting world, these images keep on filling in as standards for our developing comprehension of the climate, morals, legislative issues, and society. A few instances of the contemporary understanding of creature imagery include:

Ecological Protection: Numerous creature images have become energizing focuses for natural preservation endeavors. The polar bear, as an image of environmental change, has been utilized to advocate for ecological insurance and feasible practices.

Moral Conversations: Animal images regularly show up in conversations about morals, especially in discusses encompassing basic entitlements, animal testing, and processing plant cultivating. The utilization of creatures as images incites pondered mankind's treatment of the animals of the world collectively.

Sociopolitical Discourse: Creature imagery stays a strong device for political editorial. Illustrators and humorists frequently use creatures as metaphorical figures to investigate political occasions and figures.

Individual Strengthening: In contemporary self improvement and self-awareness, people might pick creature images as tokens of individual characteristics or desires. For example, somebody might take on the falcon as an image of vision and concentration.

Reconsidering Customs: Specialists and journalists proceed to rethink customary creature imagery in clever ways, making new understandings that resound with contemporary crowds.

9.1 Animal Motifs in Artistic Expression

Over the course of craftsmanship, creature themes have been a common and flexible topic. These themes envelop many species, from the grand lion to the sensitive butterfly, and have showed up in different types of creative articulation, including painting, figure, writing, and enriching expressions. Creatures have been portrayed in craftsmanship for different reasons, frequently conveying significant imagery, adding to tasteful sytheses, and filling in as social signifiers. This article investigates the job of creature themes in imaginative articulation, diving into the diverse implications, feel, and social importance they convey.

The Imagery of Creature Themes in Craftsmanship

Creatures have long held representative significance in human culture and workmanship. These images are frequently drawn from different sources, including folklore, religion, old stories, and the normal world, and are utilized to convey a large number of ideas and feelings. A few instances of emblematic creature themes in workmanship include:

The Lion: The lion is a strong and all inclusive image, frequently addressing strength, fortitude, and respectability. In Christian craftsmanship, it represents Christ's godlikeness and triumph over death. In antiquated Mesopotamia, it was related with goddesses and the idea of security.

The Phoenix: The phoenix, a legendary bird that is reawakened from its remains, represents reestablishment, resurrection, and interminability. It frequently shows up in workmanship as an image of trust and the pattern of life.

The Pigeon: The bird is an image of harmony, virtue, and the Essence of God in Christian workmanship. Its relationship with the tale of Noah's Ark implies the commitment of a fresh start and compromise with God.

The Snake: The snake can convey both good and unfortunate underlying meanings. In certain societies, it addresses resurrection and change, while in others, it represents trickery and fiendishness. In workmanship, it frequently shows up in subjects connected with allurement, information, and life cycles.

The Butterfly: Butterflies represent change, excellence, and the fleeting idea of life. Their lifecycle, from caterpillar to chrysalis to butterfly, fills in as a similitude for self-improvement and change.

The Elephant: Elephants represent strength, intelligence, and life span. In numerous Asian societies, the trinket is related with eminence and heavenly characteristics.

The Peacock: The peacock is an image of magnificence, eternality, and pride. In Hinduism, it is related with the goddess Lakshmi, addressing riches and thriving.

Feel of Creature Themes in Workmanship

Creature themes frequently add to the stylish characteristics of workmanship, upgrading pieces and adding profundity to visual accounts. Specialists utilize different procedures to catch the excellence and intricacy of creatures in their works:

Authenticity and Naturalism: Numerous craftsmen make progress toward a sensible or naturalistic portrayal of creatures, portraying their actual elements and ways of behaving with careful detail. This approach permits watchers to see the value in the intrinsic magnificence and unpredictability of the animals of the world collectively.

Conceptual and Emblematic Craftsmanship: A specialists use deliberation and imagery to convey the substance of creatures without exacting portrayal. For instance, Wassily Kandinsky's theoretical artistic creations frequently bring out the energy and imperativeness of creatures through non-illustrative structures and varieties.

Tasteful Allure: Creatures' actual characteristics, for example, fur examples, feathers, and lively scales, are frequently celebrated for their stylish allure. Specialists use these characteristics to make outwardly striking and paramount sytheses.

Workmanship Developments: Different craftsmanship developments have utilized creature themes to different closures. The Pre-Raphaelite Fellowship, for example, involved mind boggling and definite portrayals of creatures in their attempts to associate with nature and make a powerful tasteful.

Social Meaning of Creature Themes in Craftsmanship

Creature themes in craftsmanship habitually convey social and verifiable importance, frequently mirroring the qualities, convictions, and personalities of explicit social orders. A few instances of social importance include:

Native Craftsmanship: Native societies overall have a rich custom of consolidating creature themes in their specialty. These themes frequently address otherworldly associations, familial convictions, and natural connections inside their surroundings.

Imagery in Public Personality: Public images frequently consolidate creature themes to address the social character and upsides of a country. The bald eagle in the US, for example, represents opportunity and strength.

Profound and Strict Craftsmanship: Creature themes assume a focal part in strict and otherworldly workmanship, where they convey holy implications and convictions. Hindu craftsmanship, for instance, includes a huge number of creature gods and images, each with explicit characteristics and undertones.

Society Workmanship: People craftsmanship customs every now and again integrate creature themes to communicate social stories, values, and customs. Mexican people workmanship, for example, is known for its brilliant portrayals of creatures like the alebrijes, which frequently act as otherworldly defenders.

Beautifying Expressions: Creatures show up in a great many enlivening expressions, from materials and pottery to gems and design. These themes frequently draw from social imagery and feel, adding profundity and importance to ordinary articles.

Creature Themes in Imaginative Articulation: Verifiable Models

Creature themes have been available in workmanship for quite a long time, leaving a rich verifiable heritage. A few prominent models include:

Egyptian Pictographs: Old Egyptian craftsmanship noticeably highlighted creature themes, like the falcon, feline, and scarab bug, to convey thoughts regarding divinities, assurance, and resurrection.

Chinese Brush Painting: Chinese craftsmanship, especially conventional brush painting, frequently includes creatures like the mythical beast, crane, and koi fish, each with representative implications connected with life span, flourishing, and strength.

Archaic Bestiaries: Middle age enlightened compositions, known as bestiaries, portrayed creatures both genuine and legendary. These texts involved creatures as figurative images to convey moral illustrations and strict lessons.

Japanese Ukiyo-e Prints: Japanese ukiyo-e prints from the Edo time frame as often as possible consolidated creature themes. The woodblock print "The Incomparable Wave off Kanagawa" by Hokusai broadly includes a strong wave and Mount Fuji close by boats, representing the transient idea of life and the components' colossal power.

European Renaissance Workmanship: During the Renaissance, specialists like Leonardo da Vinci and Albrecht Dürer created itemized investigations of creatures and integrated them into their works, like Dürer's "The Rhinoceros" and da Vinci's investigations of ponies.

Contemporary Creature Themes in Imaginative Articulation

The utilization of creature themes in contemporary craftsmanship keeps on flourishing, reflecting developing points of view and worries in our quickly impacting world. A few instances of contemporary creature themes in workmanship include:

Natural Craftsmanship: because of contemporary ecological issues, specialists are utilizing creature themes to bring issues to light about living space misfortune, environmental change, and untamed life preservation. Craftsmen like Walton Passage make huge scope, exceptionally definite works of art that mix normal history with social analysis.

Road Workmanship and Spray painting: Road specialists frequently integrate creature themes into their works, utilizing them to pass on friendly messages, make outwardly striking paintings, and imbue metropolitan conditions with variety and life.

Computerized Craftsmanship and Liveliness: Advances in computerized workmanship and activity have considered the making of outwardly staggering and creative creature themes. Craftsmen and artists frequently utilize creatures to investigate the limits of the real world and dream.

Contemporary Native Craftsmanship: Native specialists keep on integrating creature themes into their works, mirroring their persevering through social associations with the normal world and the effect of colonization on native environments.

Workmanship for Social Change: Contemporary specialists utilize animal themes to remark on friendly issues, for example, basic entitlements, manufacturing plant cultivating, and the morals of involving creatures in logical examinations. These works mean to incite thought and activity.

9.2 Animals in Contemporary Literature and Media

Creatures have consistently assumed a huge part in human culture and workmanship, and this impact go on in contemporary writing and media. From books and brief tales to films, TV series, and computerized stages, creatures serve different jobs and convey a huge number of implications. Their depiction goes from reasonable to emblematic, and their presence in contemporary works mirrors our perplexing connection with the collective of animals. This exposition investigates the depiction of creatures in contemporary writing and media, featuring their imagery, social importance, and the manners in which they add to stories and subjects.

Contemporary Writing: The Creature Presence

Contemporary writing has proceeded with the practice of integrating creatures into its accounts, frequently tending to complex subjects and human-creature connections. Creators utilize various procedures to remember creatures for their works, offering alternate points of view on the creature world.

Reasonable Depictions: A few contemporary creators decide to portray creatures all things considered, giving nitty gritty and exact portrayals of their way of behaving, living spaces, and cooperations. These portrayals expect to instruct perusers about the normal world, cultivate sympathy for creatures, and feature the effect of human exercises on natural life.

For instance, Barbara Kingsolver's "Extravagant Summer" offers a clear and true depiction of the normal world, including the existences of birds, bugs, and different animals, mirroring her experience in science.

Creature Stories: lately, there has been a flood in books composed according to a creature's point of view, permitting perusers to see the world through their eyes. Well known models incorporate "The Specialty of Dashing in the Downpour" by Garth Stein, described by a canine named Enzo, and "The Call of Nature" by Jack London, told according to the point of view of a tamed canine named Buck.

Imagery and Purposeful anecdote: Contemporary writing frequently utilizes creatures emblematically or metaphorically to convey more profound significance and investigate human encounters. In Yann Martel's "Life of Pi," for example, a Bengal tiger named Richard Parker turns into an emblematic portrayal of the hero's internal conflict and endurance impulses.

Creature Promotion: Numerous contemporary creators utilize their work to advocate for creature government assistance and protection. The book "The Elephant Whisperer" by Lawrence Anthony describes the writer's encounters in safeguarding a group of damaged elephants, revealing insight into the significance of untamed life preservation and restoration.

Contemporary Media: Creatures in Film and TV

The presence of creatures in contemporary media isn't restricted to writing; film and TV have likewise assumed a critical part in depicting creatures and their importance.

Untamed life Narratives: Natural life narratives keep on enamoring crowds, teaching them about the normal world and its marvels. Prestigious producers like David Attenborough have committed their professions to displaying creatures in their living spaces, uncovering the magnificence and delicacy of the World's biological systems.

Vivified Movies: Enlivened films frequently include human creatures as focal characters. These movies, like Disney's "The Lion Ruler" and "Zootopia," utilize creature characters to convey subjects of family, kinship, social issues, and self-awareness. Humanoid attribution permits these movies to draw in with the two kids and grown-ups, stressing widespread human encounters.

Preservation and Mindfulness: Contemporary media likewise fills in as a stage for bringing issues to light about natural life protection and ecological issues. Narratives like "Blackfish" shed light on the existences of hostage orcas, provoking conversations about creature imprisonment and moral worries. "The Bay" uncovered the ruthless acts of dolphin hunting in Japan, igniting worldwide shock and activism.

Science Correspondence: TV series and narratives, for example, "Planet Earth" and "Blue Planet," join staggering cinematography with logical narrating to impart complex biological ideas. These shows illuminate the general population about environmental change, natural surroundings misfortune, and the significance of saving biodiversity.

Creature Imagery and Social Importance

Creatures in contemporary writing and media frequently convey representative and social importance, mirroring the qualities, convictions, and worries of society. A portion of these images and their implications include:

The Elephant: Elephants are many times images of solidarity, insight, and memory. They are regularly depicted in writing and media as both powerless against human abuse and strong in their battles.

The Wolf: Wolves are symbolic of opportunity, instinct, and ferocity. They frequently show up as strong and mysterious characters, addressing the untamed parts of the human mind.

The Owl: Owls represent astuteness, secret, and prescience. In writing, they habitually show up as guides, offering knowledge and direction to the hero.

The Fox: Foxes are frequently connected with shrewd and dishonesty. In writing, they are depicted as shrewd and smart, filling in as original characters in tales and folktales.

The Dolphin: Dolphins address amicability, insight, and correspondence. They are frequently used to convey subjects of compassion, association, and the significance of safeguarding marine life.

The Butterfly: Butterflies represent change, reestablishment, and the temporariness of life. They frequently show up in writing and media as analogies for self-improvement and change.

Creature Imagery in Contemporary Writing

Creature imagery in contemporary writing frequently fills in as a scaffold between the normal world and the human experience. A few contemporary models include:

"The Goldfinch" by Donna Tartt: The work of art of a goldfinch fills in as a focal theme in this novel, representing the getting through excellence and delicacy of craftsmanship and life.

"The White Tiger" by Aravind Adiga: The illustration of the white tiger fills in as a moral story for social and monetary imbalance in India, addressing the underestimated and the persecuted.

"Watership Down" by Richard Adams: This clever elements a gathering of hares on a mission for another home, with each bunny exemplifying unmistakable characteristics and character qualities. The story is a convincing investigation of courage, initiative, and the human condition.

"Life of Pi" by Yann Martel: The Bengal tiger Richard Parker addresses the hero's conflict under the surface for endurance, featuring topics of flexibility, self-revelation, and the duality of human instinct.

"The Tale of Edgar Sawtelle" by David Wroblewski: The original bases on a quiet kid and his phenomenal bond with a bunch of canines. The canines represent reliability, friendship, and the persevering through association among people and creatures.

Creature Imagery in Contemporary Media

Contemporary media likewise includes creature imagery, with creatures frequently encapsulating widespread subjects and values. Models include:

"Frantic Max: Rage Street" (2015): The film depicts a tragic reality where characters use creatures as images of opportunity and endurance. The "War Young men" love a controlling wheel as a strict image, addressing their mission for timeless life, like the manner in which warlords in the film treat their brave conflict ponies.

"The Revenant" (2015): The film involves a bear as an image of force, endurance, and flexibility. The bear assault scene turns into a strong moral story for the hero's excursion through misfortune and his will to get by.

"Okja" (2017): This film follows the narrative of a little kid and her cherished super pig, Okja. The film brings up issues about the moral treatment of creatures and the results of the meat business, making Okja an image of empathy and basic entitlements.

"Darling" (1995): The film utilizes a pig named Darling to investigate subjects of personality and beating cultural assumptions. The personality of Darling difficulties generalizations and bias taking into account only superficial factors.

Social Meaning of Creatures in Contemporary Media

Contemporary media mirrors the social meaning of creatures by tending to present day concerns and values. A few instances of social importance in contemporary media include:

Ecological Mindfulness: Numerous contemporary movies and narratives address natural issues, pushing for the assurance of jeopardized species and environments. "Blackfish" and "An Awkward Truth" center around creature government assistance and environmental change, separately, reassuring watchers to make a move.

Social Discourse: Media frequently fills in as a stage for social editorial, tending to subjects, for example, basic entitlements, manufacturing plant cultivating, and the moral treatment of creatures. Narratives like "The Inlet" uncover creature mercilessness while upholding for change.

Moral Issues: Contemporary media investigates moral predicaments including creatures, like hereditary designing, cloning, and the production of human-creature half and halves. Films like "Join" and "Never Let Me Go" bring up issues about the moral limits of logical trial and error and the outcomes of altering nature.

Human-Creature Connections: Contemporary media digs into the complicated connections among people and creatures, frequently featuring the significant close to home associations between them. "Hachi: A Canine's Story" depicts the relentless dedication of a canine to its proprietor, stressing the profundity of the human-creature security.

9.3 The Ever-Evolving Role of Animals in Modern Culture

Creatures have held a significant and getting through place in human culture, filling in as wellsprings of food, friendship, imagery, and motivation. Over the entire course of time, creatures play played different parts, from being pursued for endurance to being adored as gods, from representing temperances and indecencies to addressing contemporary worries and difficulties.

In current culture, the jobs of creatures have kept on developing, reflecting changes in human qualities, mechanical advances, and natural mindfulness. This paper investigates the consistently developing job of creatures in current culture, revealing insight into the manners in which they impact our general public, morals, and aggregate character.

Friendship and Treatment Creatures: The advancing job of creatures in current culture is maybe most apparent in the rising significance of pets and treatment creatures. As social orders have become more urbanized and innovatively driven, the friendship of creatures has taken on more noteworthy importance. For some individuals, pets offer profound help and companionship as well as a feeling of direction and obligation.

1. **Everyday reassurance Creatures:** In contemporary culture, daily encouragement creatures (ESAs) are turning out to be more common, assisting people with adapting to psychological wellness difficulties like uneasiness and discouragement. These creatures offer solace, friendship, and a quieting presence.
2. **Treatment Creatures:** Treatment creatures are utilized in different restorative settings, like medical clinics, nursing homes, and schools, to offer profound help and help in the recuperating system. Canines, specifically, are regularly utilized as treatment creatures because of their delicate nature and instinctive comprehension of human feelings.
3. **Creature Helped Treatment (AAT):** AAT includes uniquely prepared creatures working with specialists to assist people with defeating physical, close to home, and mental difficulties. Equine treatment, for instance, uses ponies to help individuals with incapacities or emotional well-being issues.

Protection and Biodiversity: Current culture has seen a developing accentuation on preservation and biodiversity conservation. As attention to the natural effect of human exercises has expanded, creatures have become significant images and diplomats for ecological causes.

1. **Preservation Symbols:** Certain creature species have become symbols of protection, bringing issues to light about the significance of safeguarding biodiversity. Species like the panda, tiger, and polar bear are significant of more extensive protection endeavors and act as images of the need to address natural surroundings misfortune and environmental change.

2. **Alluring Megafauna:** Appealling megafauna, like elephants, rhinoceroses, and whales, catch the public's consideration and rouse preservation activity. These enormous and famous creatures act as central focuses for bringing issues to light about jeopardized species and living space security.

3. **Ecological Missions:** Non-benefit associations and natural missions frequently use creatures as envoys to draw in the general population. The World Natural life Asset (WWF), for example, uses the picture of the goliath panda in its logo and marking to advance preservation endeavors around the world.

Moral Utilization and Creature Government assistance: In current culture, there is a developing worry for creature government assistance and the moral treatment of creatures. Customers are progressively aware of the beginnings of their food, apparel, and items, prompting huge changes in how creatures are raised, butchered, and utilized for different purposes.

1. **Moral Cultivating Practices:** Worries about production line cultivating, creature remorselessness, and the moral treatment of domesticated animals have driven changes in farming practices. Terms like "unfenced," "confine free," and "natural" have become related with additional accommodating and moral ways to deal with animal cultivating.

2. **Veganism and Plant-Based Diets:** Veganism and plant-based eats less have acquired prevalence as people decide to swear off creature items for plant-based other options. These dietary decisions are in many cases driven by moral worries for creature government assistance, as well as wellbeing and ecological contemplations.

3. **Creature Testing and Beauty care products:** Expanding familiarity with creature testing in the makeup business has prompted a shift toward brutality free items. Buyers are requesting choices that don't include creature trial and error, inciting many organizations to embrace more moral practices.

Basic entitlements and Legitimate Securities: The idea of basic entitlements has acquired noticeable quality in present day culture, prompting lawful assurances and contemplations for creatures that were generally neglected.

1. **Legitimate Insurances:** Various nations and locales have executed regulations and guidelines to safeguard creatures from remorselessness and misuse. These

regulations cover regions like creature mercilessness, against poaching endeavors, and the treatment of creatures in different enterprises.

2. **Backing and Activism:** Basic entitlements activists and associations, like PETA (Individuals for the Moral Treatment of Creatures), play had a significant impact in bringing issues to light about creature government assistance issues and supporting for lawful changes. Their endeavors have added to the prohibition on rehearses like prize hunting and the fur exchange a few districts.

3. **Consciousness and Personhood:** Discussions encompassing creature awareness and personhood are turning out to be progressively significant. A few nations have perceived specific creatures as conscious creatures with the ability to feel agony and experience feelings, bearing the cost of them extra legitimate insurances.

Creatures in Craftsmanship, Diversion, and Mainstream society: Creatures keep on assuming a focal part in workmanship, amusement, and mainstream society, offering amusement, motivation, and editorial on contemporary society.

1. **Energized Movies and Characters:** The depiction of creatures in vivified movies and TV series stays a valued type of diversion, offering moral illustrations and profound reverberation. Notorious characters like Simba in "The Lion Ruler" and Dory in "Tracking down Nemo" catch the minds of crowds, everything being equal.

2. **Creature Image Culture:** modern times has brought about creature image culture, where creatures like Testy Feline, Doge, and Console Feline become viral sensations. These images offer humor, critique, and social references, and they frequently bring issues to light of different issues.

3. **Protection Narratives:** Untamed life narratives, for example, those created by David Attenborough, keep on enamoring crowds by exhibiting the excellence and intricacy of the regular world. These narratives bring issues to light of the critical requirement for preservation and natural insurance.

4. **Creature Images in Workmanship:** Creature themes and images in contemporary craftsmanship keep on mirroring our relationship with the regular world and convey assorted implications. Craftsmen utilize creature symbolism to investigate issues like natural debasement, human-creature associations, and cultural qualities.

The Steadily Advancing Job of Creatures in Present day Culture: Difficulties and Contemplations

As creatures keep on advancing in their jobs in present day culture, there are a few difficulties and contemplations that society should address:

Adjusting Human and Creature Interests: The consistently developing jobs of creatures in present day culture require a fragile harmony between human interests, like horticulture, examination, and diversion, and the privileges and government assistance of creatures. Settling on something worth agreeing on that regards the interests of both is a perplexing test.

Moral Utilization and Natural Manageability: The pattern toward moral utilization and plant-based consumes less calories mirrors the craving to diminish the ecological effect of creature farming. Notwithstanding, this shift additionally brings up issues about the maintainability of plant-put together farming and its contact with respect to biological systems.

Moral Issues: Advances in biotechnology and hereditary designing have raised moral problems connected with the making of half breed creatures, cloning, and quality altering. Society should wrestle with inquiries of morals, security, and likely results.

Legitimate Assurances and Authorization: While progress has been made in the lawful security of creatures, there are continuous difficulties in implementation and worldwide norms. Facilitated endeavors and worldwide participation are expected to resolve issues like natural life dealing and creature mercilessness.

Changing Discernments and Values: The steadily advancing jobs of creatures in present day culture are intently attached to changing cultural qualities and insights. Society should explore the moving scene of moral contemplations and developing social standards.